Challenging
Brain
Boosters

Donatella Bergamino

Sterling Publishing Co., Inc.
New York

English translation by Rosa Iocono

Library of Congress Cataloging-in-Publication Data

10 9 8 7 6 5 4

Published by Sterling Publishing Co., Inc.
387 Park Avenue South, New York, NY 10016
Originally published in Italian under the title
Il Grande Libro Dei Test d'Intelligenza by
Newton & Compton editori © 2002
by Newton & Compton editori, s.r.l., Rome
Revisions and translation © 2004 by Sterling Publishing Co., Inc.
Distributed in Canada by Sterling Publishing
c/o Canadian Manda Group, One Atlantic Avenue, Suite 105
Toronto, Ontario, Canada M6K 3E7
Distributed in Great Britain by Chrysalis Books Group PLC
The Chrysalis Building, Bramley Road, London W10 6SP, England
Distributed in Australia by Capricorn Link (Australia) Pty. Ltd.
P.O. Box 704, Windsor, NSW 2756, Australia

Sterling ISBN: 1-4027-0946-3

Contents

Introduction

In response to the question, "Am I smart?" modern psychology suggests that the actual question should be, "Do I have a high IQ?"

Intelligence Quotient or IQ tests provide a fairly accurate evaluation of a person's intelligence, and the tests in this book will give the reader a useful indication of his or her IQ. We are not suggesting that these tests assess every possible form of human intelligence, but they do provide a way to measure intelligence in certain areas, e.g., verbal, numerical, and visuospatial, permitting readers to make a solid assessment of their IQ.

In the answer sections, explanations are provided that will help you with questions you were unable to answer or got wrong. By taking note of your thought processes as you take the tests and by studying the results, you will gain a better understanding of how your mind works and how to make it work better.

Before You Begin

Measuring Intelligence

Various methods exist to calculate intelligence. Many tests have a standard procedure and calculate the result in terms of deviation and distance from (above and below) the median. The fixed median is usually 100. Other tests count the number of questions and calculate IQ by the number of correct responses. The median equals approximately half the number of attempts.

This book measures the score of each of three forms of intelligence, defined by modern psychology as verbal, numeric, and spatial intelligence. The eight tests in Part 1 incorporate a variety of questions. They are followed in Part 2 by three tests designed to measure specific types of intelligence and reasoning, and a fourth test that is advanced but more general.

The verbal test contains questions covering anagrams, knowledge of general culture, word completion, and missing letters. The numerical test measures the ability to calculate and to use inductive and deductive reasoning. The spatial test calls for good eyesight and attention to detail to determine differences among figures.

Taking the Tests

To answer the different types of questions and achieve a good score:

1. Allow 50 minutes for each test. It may help to have someone who is not taking the test time you. If that is not possible, use a stopwatch or timer.
2. Don't allow anyone to disturb you or help you during the tests.
3. The tests contain questions that call for thinking. Don't look at the questions before taking the tests. This will not benefit you and will invalidate your score.
4. After finishing one test, wait at least half an hour before taking another. You will be more relaxed and your mind will be more focused on the upcoming test.
5. Before taking a test, reread these instructions to refresh your memory. During the test, take the time to read each question carefully; this will keep you from wasting time on incorrect answers.

Types of Questions

1. Numeric patterns (find the next number in a series or find the missing number)
2. Letter patterns (find the next word in a series or find the missing word)
3. Numeric, letter, and verbal analogies (i.e., A is to B as A' is to ?)
4. Find the letter or number (complete the word or number pattern)
5. Word anagrams (unscramble words or select the word that doesn't belong or that should be included)
6. Spatial relations (find the next figure in a series or the one that doesn't belong)

Not only will these tests help determine your IQ, but they are also good mind-stimulating exercises.

Good luck!

Part 1

Measuring Your Intelligence

Test 1

1. **What is the missing month?**

   Scorpio:November::Leo:...

   A. September
   B. August
   C. May
   D. June
   E. April

2. **Find the missing number.**

   1   4   3   7   5   10   7   ...

3. **Unscramble the following letters to find the word that is not a flower.**

   A. ylli
   B. tnorcaian
   C. iadys
   D. ltpui
   E. koa

4. **Find the missing number.**

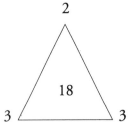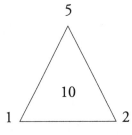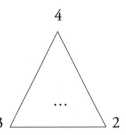

5. Which name does not belong?

A. Verdi
B. Wagner
C. Rossini
D. Puccini
E. Dvorak

6. Find the missing number.

2	8
4	6

10	4
4	2

5	1
4	...

7. Choose the correct response.

All animals are mammals.

A. definitely true
B. not true
C. sometimes true
D. an opinion

8. Which figure does not belong?

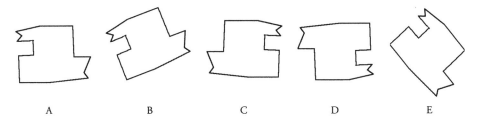

A   B   C   D   E

9. Find the missing number.

5   3   8   6   11   ...   14   12

10. Complete the series with the correct word.

Small base
Height
Large base
Oblique side
…
A. trapezoid   B. triangle   C. rectangle   D. rhombus   E. circle

11. Find the missing number.

1   2   3   7   …

12. Which word is not a synonym of the others?

A.   savage
B.   untamed
C.   misanthropic
D.   feral
E.   wild

13. Find the missing letter.

A   C   E   G   I   …

14. Find the word that can precede each of these words to form new words.

Word
Key
Port

15. Find the missing number.

6-4-2   5-4-3   4-2-…

16. Find the word that means the same thing as each of the other two.

Thorax (….) Bureau

17. Find the missing number.

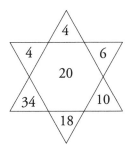 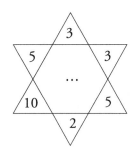

18. Find the missing number.

  1   2   4   8   16   32   ...

19. Which term is the most appropriate?

To pick out a person or thing by its identity:

A. to discover   B. to identify   C. to investigate

20. Which figure does not belong?

 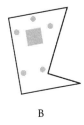   

   A   B   C   D   E

21. Find the missing number.

3	5	7
6	4	2
3	...	1

22. Insert the correct figure.

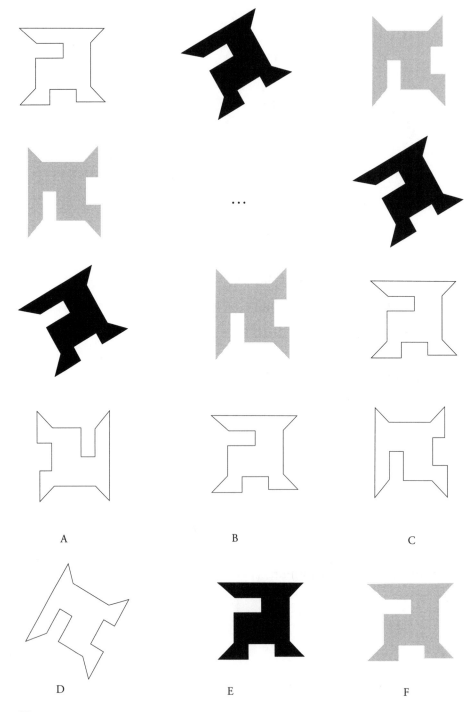

23. Find the missing number.

718   (68)   582

474   ( )   226

24. Which two words are similar?

A. Viennese
B. Siamese
C. Japanese
D. Pekingese
E. Burmese

25. Find the missing number.

718   (16)   556

474   ( )   681

26. Find the missing number.

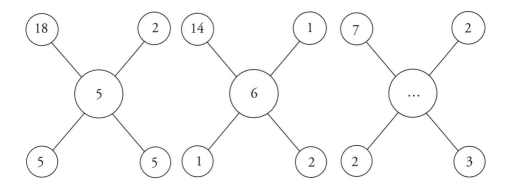

27. Which word is not a synonym of the others?

A. motionless
B. still
C. fixed
D. broken
E. immobile

28. What is the next figure in the series?

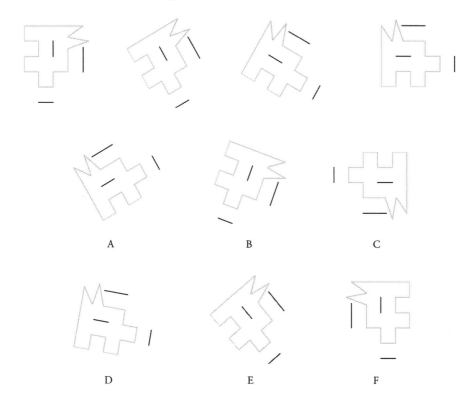

A   B   C

D   E   F

29. What is the missing number?

3:6::13:...

A. 9 B. 26 C. 69 D. 20 E. 50

30. What is the missing word?

Red:blood::green:...

A. rainbow
B. sky
C. grass
D. sea
E. street

31. Find the missing number.

  1   4   10   22   46   94   ...

32. What is the missing figure?

 : :: :

  A   B   C   D

33. Find the missing number.

  39   40   42   45   49   54   60   ...

34. Which word does not belong?

A. always
B. never
C. go
D. often
E. slowly

35. Find the missing letter.

  C-B-B   D-B-A   A-E-...

36. Find the missing number.

  7   24   31   55   86   ...

37. Find the missing number.

19	(10)	64
87	(15)	96
43	( )	52

38. Unscramble the following letters to find the word that is not a month.

A. dsutyae
B. rujynaa
C. iplra
D. yujl
E. beertemps

39. Find the missing number.

3	9	3
2	...	2
3	6	2

40. Complete the series with the correct word.

Choose
Send
Annoy
Come
...
A. boy   B. vegetable   C. close   D. always   E. pencil

41. Which number does not belong?

20   18   14   11   12   16

42. Rearrange the numbers from smallest to largest.

0.55   3/4   2/4   0.6   1/100

43. Insert the correct figure.

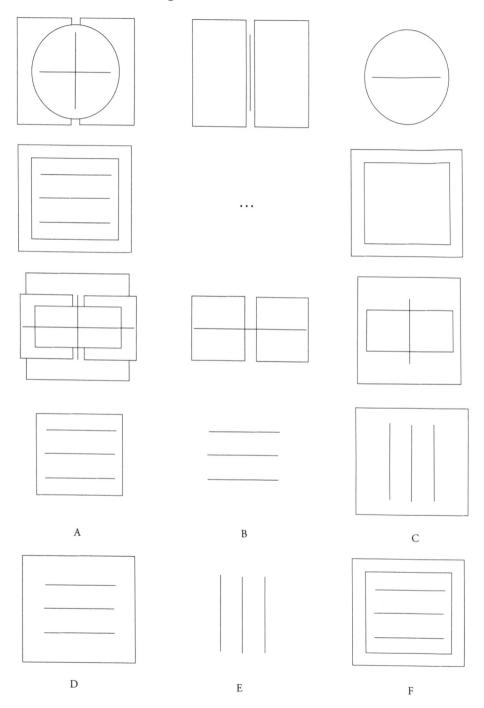

A

B

C

D

E

F

44. Which figure does not belong?

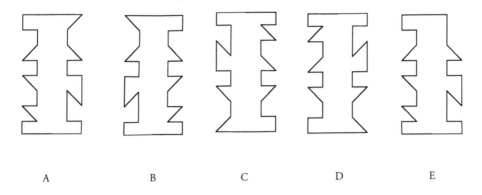

A   B   C   D   E

45. Which two names are similar?

A. Diana   B. Artemis   C. Hera   D. Athena   E. Juno

46. Find the missing number.

5   7   6   8   7   ...

47. Find the word that means the same thing as each of the other two.

Topic (....) Expose

48. Find the missing number.

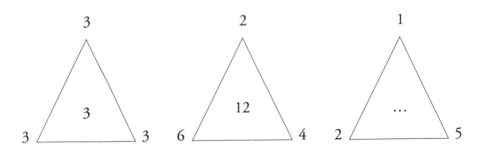

49. What is the next figure in the series?

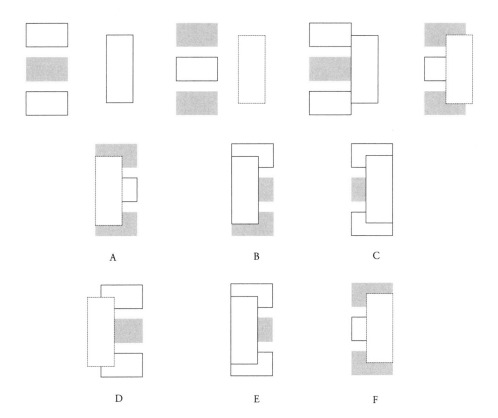

A   B   C

D   E   F

50. Unscramble the following letters to find the word that is not a country.

A. dnwtsilezar
B. ytail
C. letseat
D. anrcfe
E. aisler

Answers

1. B; August. (This is the month that corresponds to the zodiacal sign Leo.)
2. 13. (There are two alternating series; the first increases by 2 and the second by 3.)
3. E; oak. (This is a tree; lily, carnation, daisy, and tulip are flowers.)
4. 24. (Calculate the product of the external numbers.)
5. E; Dvorak. (He composed symphonies, not operas.)
6. 10. (The sum of the numbers is always 20.)
7. B.
8. C. (The figure is reversed.)
9. 9. (The series alternately subtracts 2 and adds 5.)
10. A; trapezoid. (All the parts are elements of a trapezoid.)
11. 22. (Calculate the product of the first and second numbers, the second and third, the third and fourth, etc., and add 1.)
12. C; misanthropic.
13. K. (The series always skips one letter.)
14. The word "pass" may be added before the three words to form three new words.
15. 6. (The sum of each series is always 12.)
16. Chest.
17. 8. (Calculate the difference between the sums of the numbers in each of the two large triangles that form the star.)
18. 64. (The series progressively doubles.)
19. B; to identify.
20. E. (The figure is reversed.)
21. 2. (Calculate the sum of the external numbers and divide by 2.)
22. B. (Every row has a white figure, a black figure, and a gray figure, always at the same angles.)
23. 124. (Calculate the difference between the number in the left column and the right column and divide by two.)
24. B and E, Siamese and Burmese, respectively. (They are two breeds of cat.)
25. 15. (Calculate the sum of the individual digits of one of the outside numbers.)

26. 2. (Calculate the difference between the sum of the numbers in the upper circles and the sum of the numbers in the lower circles and divide by two.)
27. D; broken.
28. A. (The figure rotates counterclockwise 30 degrees.)
29. B; 26. (The second number doubles the first.)
30. C; grass.
31. 190. (The series increases by 3, 6, 12, 24, 48, and 96 and each interval doubles progressively.)
32. D.
33. 67. (The series progressively increases by 1, 2, 3, etc.)
34. C; go. (This is a verb; the others are all adverbs.)
35. A. (The sum of the numerical equivalents of the letters in each series is always 7.)
36. 141. (Calculate the sum of the first and second numbers, the second and third, the third and fourth, etc.)
37. 7. (It is the sum of the individual digits of one of the outside numbers.)
38. A; Tuesday. (This is a day of the week; January, April, July, and September are months.)
39. 4. (Calculate the product of the external numbers in the rows.)
40. C; close. (This is the only verb.)
41. 11. (It's the only odd number.)
42. 1/100 (0.001), 2/4 (0.50), 0.55, 0.60, 3/4 (0.75).
43. B. (Subtract the third figure from the first.)
44. E. (The shape is different.)
45. A and E, Diana and Juno, respectively. (They are Roman goddesses; the others are all Greek goddesses.)
46. 9. (The series alternates by adding 2 and subtracting 1.)
47. Subject.
48. 10. (Calculate the product of the numbers in the lower angles and divide by the number in the upper angle.)
49. C. (The right-hand rectangle moves gradually left and the colors of the left-hand rectangles alternate between gray and white.)
50. C; Seattle. (This is a city; Switzerland, Italy, France, and Israel are countries.)

Test 2

1. What is the missing word?

France:French::Hungary:...

A. Persian
B. Hungarian
C. Foreign
D. Famished
E. Croatian

2. Find the missing number.

13   19   25   31   37   43   ...

3. Unscramble the letters to find the word that is not a sport.

A. lsebalba
B. nfgince
C. rkdbsnaiaetog
D. berka
E. nxgobi

4. Find the missing number.

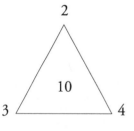
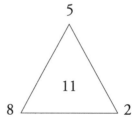
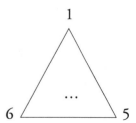

5. **Find the missing number.**

   5   7   6   8   7   9   8   ...

6. **Which two words are similar?**

   A. always B. go C. between   D. often   E. ugly

7. **Find the missing number.**

1	8
2	4

7	56
14	28

5	40
10	...

8. **Find the missing numbers.**

   5   1   9   6   17   16

9. **Choose the correct response.**

   All astrologers are graduates.

   A.   definitely true
   B.   not true
   C.   sometimes true
   D.   an opinion

10. **Which word is not a synonym of the others?**

   A.   join
   B.   affiliate
   C.   congregate
   D.   inscribe
   E.   associate

11. Which figure does not belong?

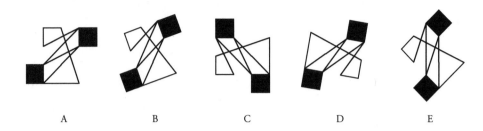

A   B   C   D   E

12. Complete the series with the correct word.

Penguin
Seal
Musk ox
Walrus
...
A. red fox   B. polar bear   C. lion   D. cat   E. salmon

13. Find the missing number

6   9   9   15   12   21   15   ...

14. Find the missing letter.

L-E-C   H-A-K   O-B-...

15. Find the missing number.

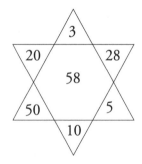   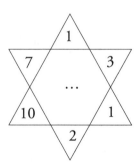

16. Find the word that means the same thing as each of the other two.

Present (....) Flow

17. Find the missing number.

10-13-3   16-...-1   20-25-5

18. Which figure does not belong?

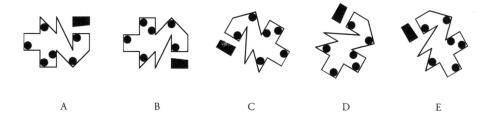

A   B   C   D   E

19. Unscramble the following letters to find the word that is not an item used in the kitchen.

A.   rofk
B.   nosop
C.   shkwi
D.   iamcrhra
E.   redshawish

20. Find the missing number.

2	15	17
10	12	...
8	7	15

21. Which two words are similar?

A. bulldog   B. celery   C. Pekingese   D. race   E. China

22. Find the missing number.

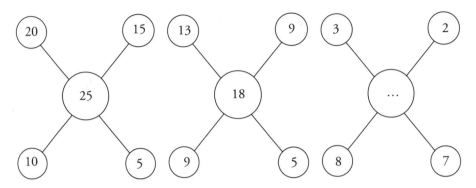

23. What is the missing number?

4:16::10:...

A. 25   B. 20   C. 75   D. 100   E. 30

24. Find the missing number.

12   11   18   14   24   17   ...

25. Which word is not a synonym of the others?

A.   sluggish
B.   lazy
C.   slothful
D.   indolent
E.   scared

26. Find the missing letter.

A   C   F   J   O   ...

27. Which number does not belong?

10   18   17   36   40   100

28. Insert the correct figure.

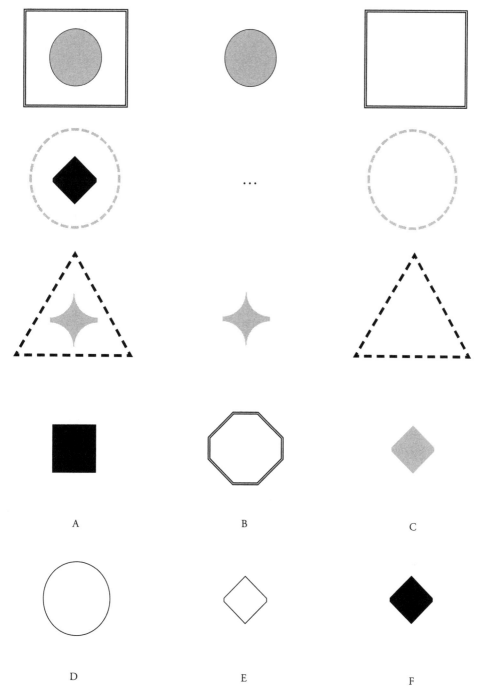

A   B   C

D   E   F

29. What is the next figure in the series?

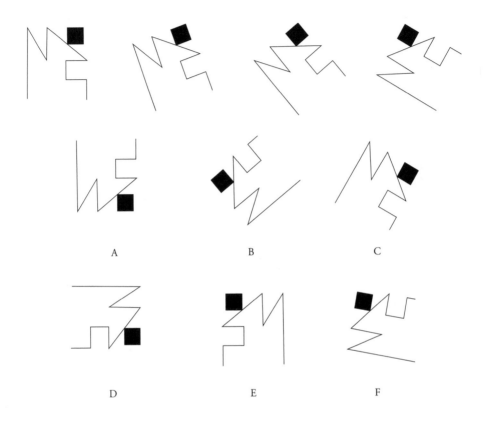

A   B   C

D   E   F

30. Which two words are similar?

A. celebrate
B. reminisce
C. officiate
D. congregate
E. discuss

31. Find the missing number.

10   100   10

4   5

8   24   3

32. Complete the series with the correct word.

Mouth
Nose
Cheeks
Chin
...

A. hands   B. feet   C. forehead   D. stomach   E. breasts

33. Find the missing number.

2   5   3   7   4   9   5   11   ...

34. Find the missing letter.

B-M-E   D-I-G   L-...-C

35. Unscramble the following letters to find the word that is not a tree.

A.   koa
B.   lepma
C.   prolap
D.   rntacanoi
E.   lowilw

36. Which two numbers are similar?

A. 16   B. 7   C. 86   D. 13   E. 42

37. Find the missing number.

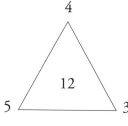 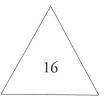 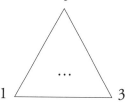

38. What is the missing figure?

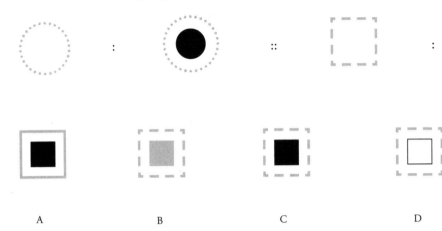

| A | B | C | D |

39. Find the word that means the same thing as each of the other two.

Narrative (....) Unique

40. Rearrange the numbers from smallest to largest.

0.05   1/5   1/2   0.60   0.25

41. Which word does not belong?

A.   horrible
B.   horrendous
C.   disgusting
D.   dirty
E.   nauseating

42. Find the missing letter.

J   M   P   S   ...

43. Find the missing number.

63   35   59   30   55   25   51   ...

44. Insert the correct figure.

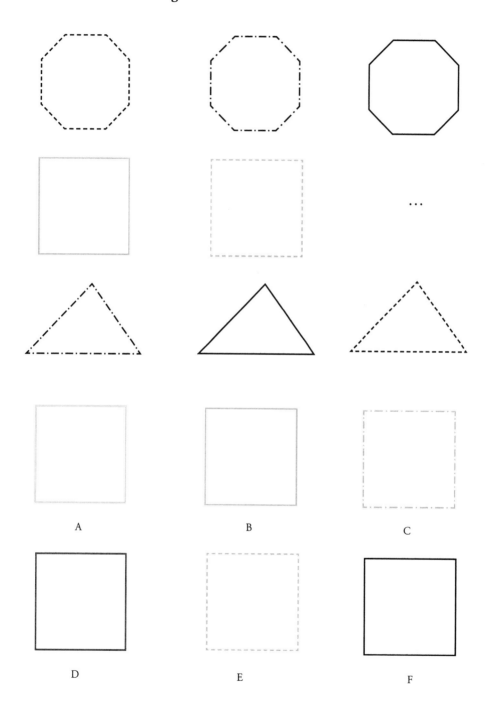

45. What is the next figure in the series?

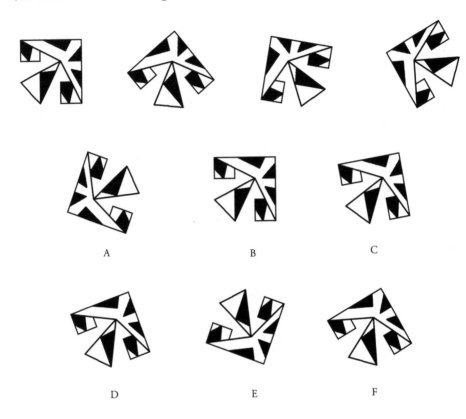

A   B   C

D   E   F

46. Unscramble the following letters to find the word that is not a fruit.

   A.   anaban
   B.   teanaplouc
   C.   etltecu
   D.   gnareinet
   E.   cheap

47. Find the missing number.

925   (307)   311

911   (   )   823

48. What is the missing word?

Dock:boat::station::...

A. train
B. engineer
C. locomotive
D. railroad
E. tracks

49. Which figure does not belong?

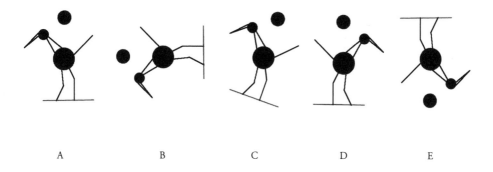

A   B   C   D   E

50. What is the missing number?

24:6::32:...

A. 30   B. 18   C. 8   D. 62   E. 38

Answers

1. B; Hungarian.
2. 49. (The series increases by 6.)
3. D; baker. (This is an occupation; baseball, fencing, skateboarding, and boxing are sports.)
4. 29. (Multiply the numbers at the base and subtract the number at the upper angle.)
5. 10. (The series alternately adds 2 and subtracts 1.)
6. A and D, always and often, respectively. (They are adverbs.)
7. 20. (The number doubles in each square moving counterclockwise.)
8. 13 and 11. (There are two alternating series; the first increases by 4 and the second by 5.)
9. B.
10. D; inscribe.
11. D. (The figure is reversed.)
12. B; polar bear. (They are all animals that live in polar areas.)
13. 27. (There are two alternating series; the first increases by 3 and the second by 6.)
14. C. (The sum of the numerical equivalent of the letters in each series is always 20.)
15. 12. (Calculate the sum of the numbers in the angles of each large triangle.)
16. Current.
17. 17. (Calculate the sum of the first and third numbers.)
18. B. (The figure is reversed.)
19. D; armchair. (This is used in the living room; fork, spoon, whisk, and dishwasher are used in the kitchen.)
20. 22. (Add the first and second numbers.)
21. A and C, bulldog and Pekingese, respectively. (These are types of dogs.)
22. 10. (Add the numbers in the circles diagonally opposite.)
23. D; 100. (The number is squared.)
24. 30. (There are two alternating series; the first increases by 6 and the second by 3.)
25. E; scared.

26. U. (The series skips one letter, then two letters, then three letters, etc.)
27. 17. (This is the only odd number.)
28. F. (Subtract the second figure from the first.)
29. F. (The figure rotates 20 degrees counterclockwise.)
30. A and C, celebrate and officiate, respectively. (Both indicate presiding at an event.)
31. 20. (Calculate the product of the first and third number in the row.)
32. C; forehead. (They are all parts of the face.)
33. 6. (There are two alternating series; the first increases by 1 and the second by 2.)
34. E. (The sum of the numerical equivalent of the letters in each series is always 20.)
35. D; carnation. (This is a flower; oak, maple, poplar, and willow are trees.)
36. B and D, 7 and 13, respectively. (Both of these are odd numbers.)
37. 19. (Calculate the sum of the numbers of each angle of the triangle.)
38. C.
39. Novel.
40. 0.05, 1/5 (0.20), 0.25, 1/2 (0.50) 0.60.
41. D; dirty.
42. V. (The series always skips two letters.)
43. 20. (There are two alternating series; the first decreases by 4 and the second by 5.)
44. C. (There are always three different outlines in each column and row.)
45. A. (The figure rotates 40 degrees counterclockwise.)
46. C; lettuce. (This is a vegetable; banana, cantaloupe, tangerine, and peach are fruits.)
47. 44. (Calculate the difference between numbers in the outside columns and divide by 2.)
48. A; train.
49. D. (The figure is reversed.)
50. C; 8. (It's one quarter of the first number.)

Test 3

1. What is the missing word?

Finger:hand::tooth:…

A. foot
B. tongue
C. mouth
D. face
E. lip

2. Find the missing number

6   3   12   6   18   9   24   12   30   …

3. Find the missing number.

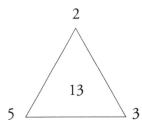 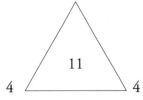 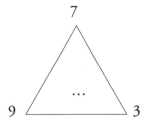

4. Choose the correct response.

If I am an engineer, I am methodical.

A. definitely true
B. not true
C. sometimes true
D. an opinion

5. **Find the missing number.**

2	54
6	18

3	81
9	27

7	189
21	...

6. **Find the missing number.**

7   2   11   7   15   12   19   17   ...

7. **Which figure does not belong?**

A   B   C   D   E

8. **What is the missing number?**

40:10::100:...

A. 300   B. 20   C. 25   D.50   E. 400

9. **Which word is not a synonym of the others?**

A. grieving
B. disheartened
C. neurotic
D. tormented
E. distraught

10. Find the missing number.

48   82   42   79   36   76   30   73   ...

11. Which term is the most appropriate?

Ancient percussion instrument similar to a plate.

A. cymbal   B. lyre   C. sitar

12. Find the missing number.

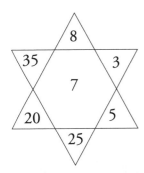 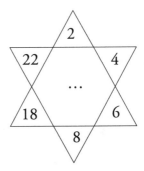

13. Find the word that means the same thing as each of the other two.

Vessel (....) Dispatch

14. Find the missing number.

12-6-3   8-4-2   24-12-...

15. Which color does not belong?

A.   violet
B.   blue
C.   indigo
D.   yellow
E.   green

16. Insert the correct figure.

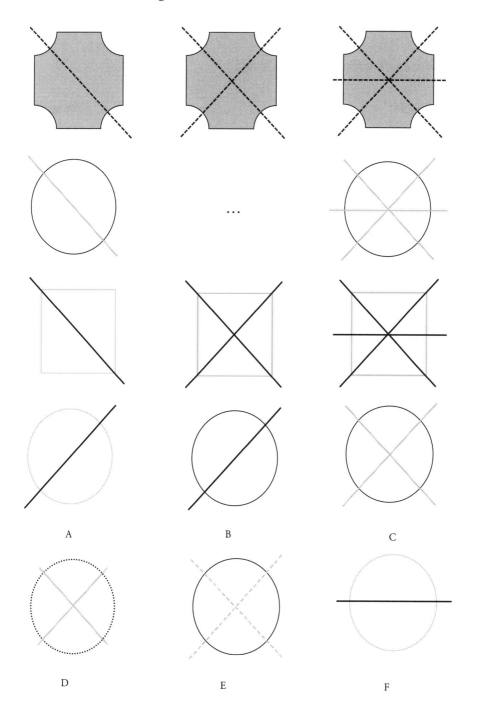

17. Find the missing number.

19   15   17   12   15   ...   13   6

18. Which figure does not belong?

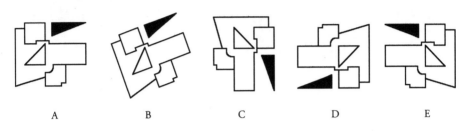

A   B   C   D   E

19. Find the word that means the same thing as each of the other two.

Cast off (....) Lean-to

20. Find the missing letter.

C-C-C   E-C-A   D-B-...

21. Unscramble the following letters to find the word that is not an insect.

A.   citkcre
B.   peanetlh
C.   ngta
D.   ayldrnfog
E.   quotismo

22. Find the missing number.

23   18   13

24   19   ...

11   6   1

23. What is the next figure in the series?

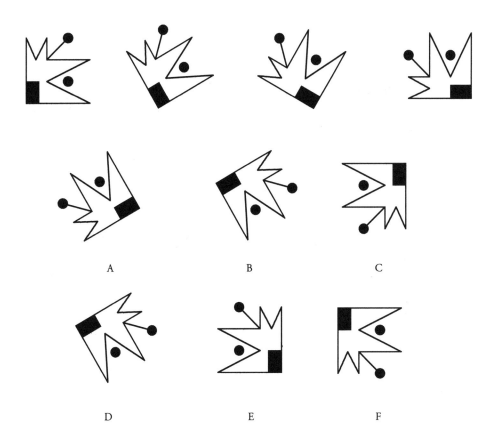

24. Find the missing number.

800   (50)   750

650   ( )   600

25. Which two words are similar?

A. order   B. comfort   C. laziness   D. serenity   E. solace

26. Find the missing number.

3   6   11   15   19   24   27   33   ...

27. Which name does not belong?

A. P.D. James
B. Dorothy L. Sayers
C. Ursula K. Le Guin
D. Sue Grafton
E. Agatha Christie

28. Find the missing number.

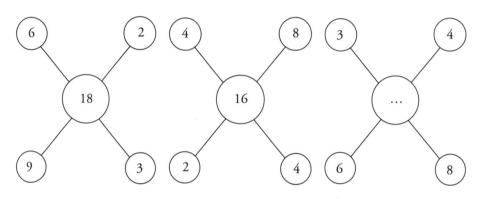

29. Which two words are similar?

A. brother   B. bond   C. love   D. tie   E. friendship

30. Find the missing number.

5   8   6   9   7   10   8   ...

31. Find the word that means the same thing as each of the other two.

Safe (....) Obtain

32. Find the missing number.

440   (8)   530

700   ( )   250

33. What is the missing figure?

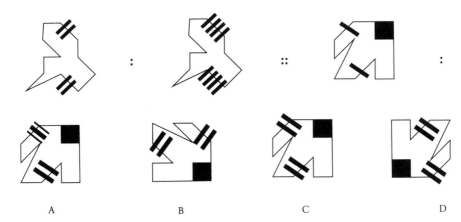

| A | B | C | D |

34. Which word is not a synonym of the others?

A. joke
B. bon mot
C. jest
D. fraud
E. witticism

35. Unscramble the following letters to find the word that is not a fish.

A. lmsnao
B. ipgunen
C. insarde
D. lrednouf
E. urtto

36. What is the missing number?

15:45::22:...

A. 32   B. 45   C. 50   D. 66   E. 16

37. Rearrange the numbers from largest to smallest.

0.5   1/4   3/5   0.8   0.06

38. Complete the series with the correct word.

Dolphin
Manatee
Otter
Shark
...
A. whale   B. pirannah   C. seal   D. penguin   E. salmon

39. Find the missing number.

77   85   93   101   109   ...

40. What is the missing word?

25:Christmas::1:...

A. Easter
B. New Year
C. Party
D. January
E. Year

41. Find the missing number.

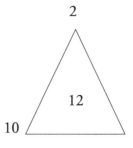 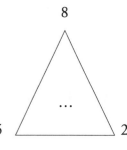

42. Insert the correct figure.

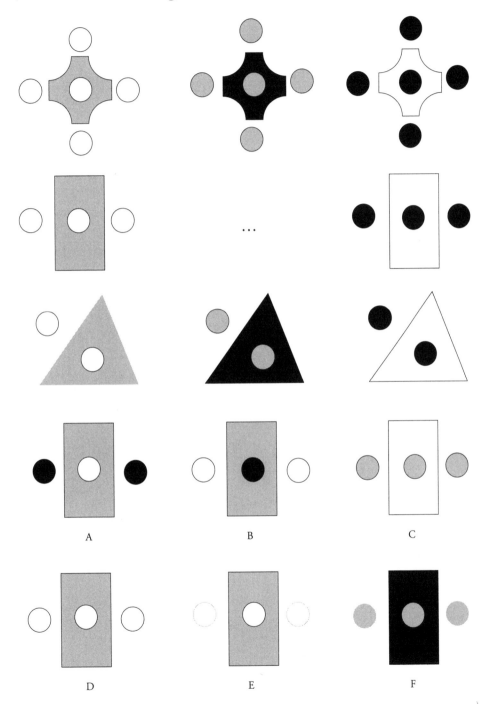

43. What is the next figure in the series?

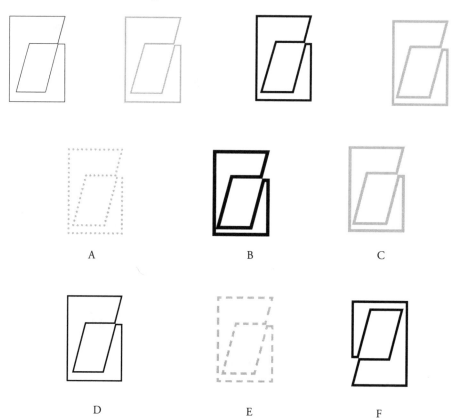

44. Find the missing number.

9   11   8   9   7   7   6   5   ...

45. Unscramble the following letters to find the word that is not a vegetable.

A. eltutce
B. dcoirhaic
C. ntleil
D. evnied
E. recyle

46. Find the missing number.

63   35   57   32   51   29   ...

47. Unscramble the following letters to find the word that is not an occupation.

- A.   cdtoro
- B.   lryewa
- C.   rtasti
- D.   vneisetoli
- E.   rcsaets

48. Find the missing number.

15   17   16   18   17   19   18   ...

49. Find the missing number.

5   13   9

22   ...   26

12   20   16

50. Which figure does not belong?

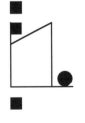 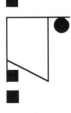 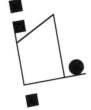  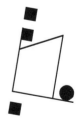

A   B   C   D   E

Answers

1. C; mouth.
2. 15. (There are two alternating series; the first increases by 6 and the second by 3.)
3. 20. (Multiply the numbers at the base and subtract the number at the vertex.)
4. D.
5. 63. (Multiply by 3 moving counterclockwise.)
6. 23. (There are two alternating series; the first increases by 4 and the second by 5.)
7. E. (The figure is reversed.)
8. C; 25. (They are each one quarter of the other number.)
9. C; neurotic.
10. 24. (There are two alternating series; the first decreases by 6 and the second by 3.)
11. A; cymbal.
12. 10. (Subtract the smaller numbers from the larger one in each large triangle.)
13. Ship.
14. 6. (Each successive number is divided by 2.)
15. D; yellow. (Yellow is a warm color and the others are cool.)
16. C. (The lines increase progressively.)
17. 9. (There are two alternating series; the first decreases by 2 and the second by 3.)
18. E. (The figure is reversed.)
19. Shed.
20. C. (The sum of the numerical equivalent of the letters in each series is always 9.)
21. B; elephant. (This is a mammal; cricket, gnat, dragonfly, and mosquito are insects.)
22. 14. (The difference between any two consecutive numbers in a row is always 5.)
23. A. (The figure rotates 30 degrees counterclockwise.)
24. 50. (Calculate the difference between the two outer numbers.)
25. B and E, comfort and solace, respectively.

26. 35. (There are two alternating series; the first increases by 8 and the second by 9.)
27. C; Ursula K. Le Guin. (She's a science fiction writer; the others are all mystery writers.)
28. 24. (Calculate the product of the numbers in the circles diagonally opposite.)
29. B and D, bond and tie, respectively.
30. 11. (The series alternates by adding 3 and subtracting 2.)
31. Secure.
32. 7. (This is the sum of the individual digits of each outside number.)
33. C. (Add an oblique line to each existing line.)
34. D; fraud.
35. B; penguin. (This is a bird; salmon, sardine, flounder, and trout are fish.)
36. D; 66. (The number is tripled.)
37. 0.80, 3/5 (0.60), 0.50, 1/4 (0.25), 0.06.
38. A; whale. (The words are in alphabetical order.)
39. 117. (The series increases by 8.)
40. B; New Year.
41. 24. (Calculate the difference between the lower angles and multiply by the corresponding number of the upper angle.)
42. F. (In each series, the figures are white and gray, gray and black, and white and black.)
43. B. (The line increases in width and alternates gray and black.)
44. 5. (There are two alternating series; the first decreases by 1 and the second by 2.)
45. C; lentil. (This is a legume; lettuce, radicchio, endive, and celery are vegetables.)
46. 45. (There are two alternating series; the first decreases by 6 and the second by 3.)
47. D; television. (This is a home appliance; doctor, lawyer, artist, and actress are occupations.)
48. 20. (The series alternates by adding 2 and subtracting 1.)
49. 30. (Calculate the sum of the first two numbers and divide by 2.)
50. B. (The figure is reversed.)

Test 4

1. Find the missing number.

   1   4   7   10   13   ...

2. Unscramble the following letters to find the word that is not a three-dimensional object.

A. nrgeliat
B. perhes
C. buce
D. ylderinc
E. ncoe

3. Find the missing number.

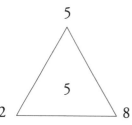
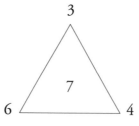
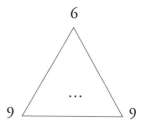

4. Which two words are similar?

A. lobster   B. clam   C. crab   D. mullet   E. porch

5. Find the missing numbers.

   1   4   7   7   19   13

6. Find the word that means the same thing as each of the other two.

Fasten (....) Draw

7. Find the missing number.

5	13
11	7

12	10
6	8

14	5
1	...

8. Which term is the most appropriate?

One who is very engaged at work.

A. diligent   B. serious   C. confident

9. Which figure does not belong?

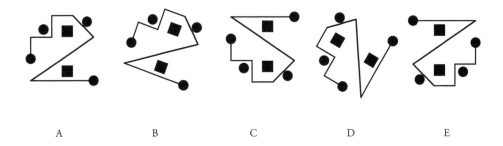

| A | B | C | D | E |

10. What is the missing number?

18:6::57:...

A. 8   B. 55   C. 19   D. 22   E. 30

11. Find the missing number.

48   52   44   47   40   ...   36   37

12. Which word is not a synonym of the others?

A. evil
B. wicked
C. treacherous
D. tormented
E. villainous

13. Find the missing number.

65   15   59   12   53   9   ...

14. Find the missing number.

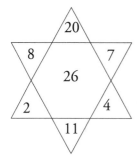 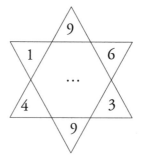

15. Which word does not belong?

A   bathing suit
B. sandals
C. Bermuda shorts
D. coat
E. clogs

16. Find the missing number

20-4-8   10-5-5   9-6-...

17. Insert the correct figure.

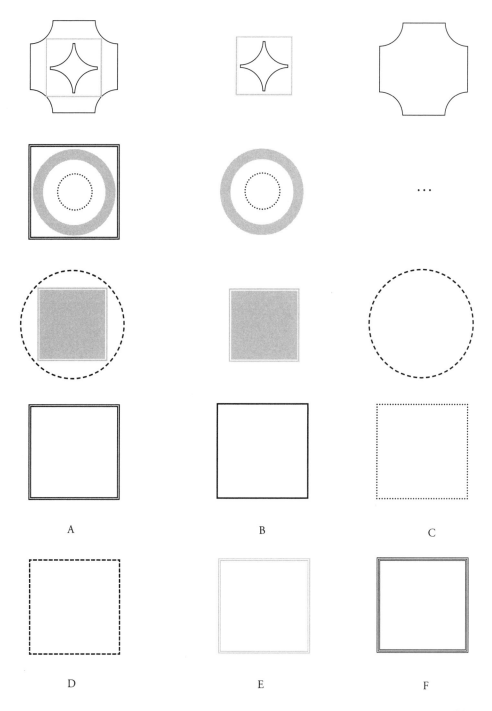

A

B

C

D

E

F

18. Which figure does not belong?

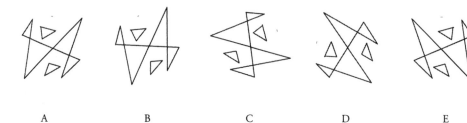

A   B   C   D   E

19. Which word does not belong?

A. barley   B. wheat   C. oat   D. rice   E. peanut

20. Find the missing number.

20   (60)   3

15   ( )   8

21. Find the word that means the same thing as each of the other two.

Rafter (....) Grin

22. Find the missing number.

10   8   8   5   6   2   4   ...

23. Unscramble the following letters to find the word that is not a breed of cat.

A. amesies
B. mtadlnaai
C. sruebme
D. snaperi
E. inanybasis

24. What is the missing number?

5:10::3:...

A. 9   B. 6   C. 10   D. 7   E. 8

25. Complete the series with the correct word.

McKinley
Kilimanjaro
Blanc
Everest

...

A. K2   B. Peak   C. Tiber   D. Sahara   E. mountain

26. What is the next figure in the series?

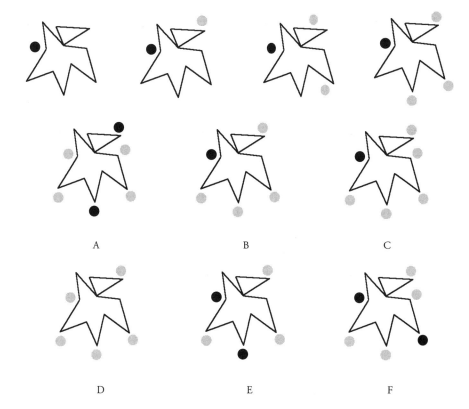

A   B   C

D   E   F

27. Find the missing number.

   4   10   16   22   28   34   40   ...

28. Which two words are similar?

   A. myrtle   B. tangerine   C. thyme   D. cherry   E. grass

29. Find the missing number.

   500   (73)   427

   383   (98)   285

   948   ( )   641

30. Which word is not a synonym of the others?

   A.   blizzard
   B.   sirocco
   C.   zephyr
   D.   gale
   E.   breeze

31. Find the missing number.

   5   3   8   6   11   9   ...

32. Find the missing number.

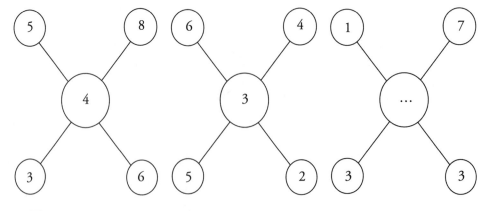

33. Insert the correct figure.

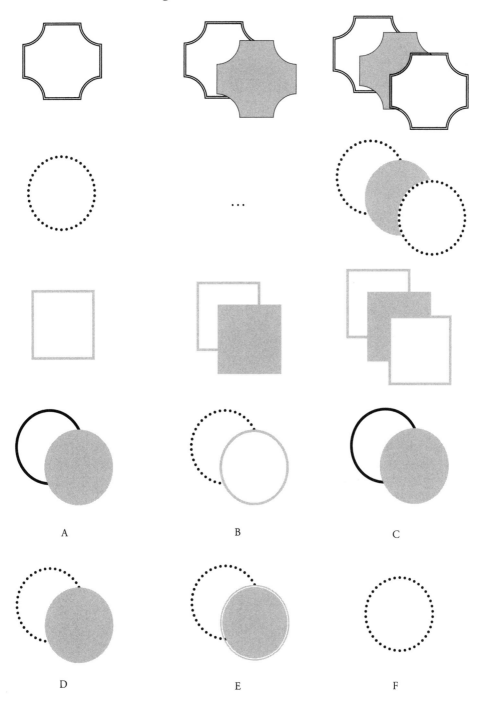

A

B

C

D

E

F

34. What is the missing figure?

 : :: :

A   B   C   D

35. Which two words are similar?

A. rested   B. comfortable   C. refreshed   D. long-lived   E. crooked

36. Find the missing number.

260   (2)   130
390   ( )   130

37. What is the missing word?

Car:steering wheel::bicycle:...

A.   seat
B.   handlebars
C.   racetrack
D.   wheel
E.   spoke

38. Rearrange the numbers from smallest to largest.

0.2   3/8   2/5   8/10   0.05

39. Find the word that means the same thing as each of the other two.

Spouse (....) Conserve

40. Find the missing number.

   4   7   5   8   6   9   7   ...

41. Unscramble the following letters to find the name that is not a woman's.

    A.   ncersaf
    B.   nejna
    C.   urlaa
    D.   tvsene
    E.   amira

42. Find the missing number.

4	20	5
2	16	...
8	24	3

43. Which figure does not belong?

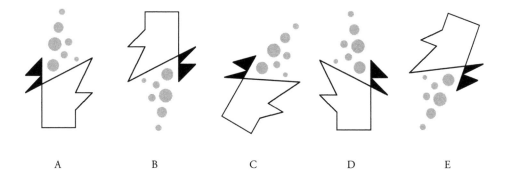

   A   B   C   D   E

44. Find the missing number

25   28   27   30   29   32   ...

45. Find the missing number.

15   4   11

23   ...   14

38   7   31

46. Find the missing number.

0   6   6   12   18   ...

47. Unscramble the following letters to find the fairy tale name that does not belong.

A. hamulinbet
B. zapernul
C. lendaricel
D. spllitskuminert
E. scolgidolk

48. Find the missing number.

7   2   11   7   15   12   ...

49. Find the missing number.

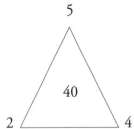
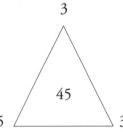
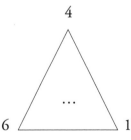

50. What is the next figure in the series?

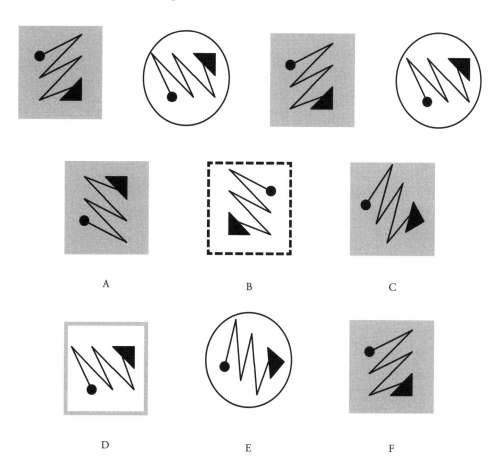

Answers

1. 16. (The series increases by 3.)
2. A; triangle. (This is a two-dimensional figure; sphere, cube, cylinder, and cone are three dimensional.)
3. 12. (Calculate the sum of the numbers at the base of the triangle and subtract the number at the vertex.)
4. A and C, lobster and crab, respectively. (They are both crustaceans.)
5. 13 and 10. (There are two alternating series; the first increases by 6 and the second by 3.)
6. Tie.
7. 16. (The sum of the numbers in the boxes is always 36.)
8. A; diligent.
9. C. (The figure is reversed.)
10. C; 19. (This is one-third of the preceding number.)
11. 42. (There are two alternating series; the first decreases by 4 and the second by 5.)
12. D; tormented.
13. 47. (There are two alternating series; the first decreases by 6 and the second by 3.)
14. 16. (Calculate the sum of the numbers in the larger triangles.)
15. D; coat. (This is not an item of summer clothing.)
16. 5. (Calculate the sum of the first and second number and divide the result by 3.)
17. A. (Subtract the second figure from the first.)
18. E. (The figure is reversed.)
19. E; peanut. (This is not a grain.)
20. 120. (Calculate the product of the outer numbers.)
21. Beam.
22. -1. (There are two alternating series; the first decreases by 2 and the second by 3.)
23. B; Dalmatian. (This is a breed of dog; Siamese, Burmese, Persian, and Abyssinian are breeds of cats.)
24. B; 6. (The first number is doubled.)
25. A; K2. (They are all mountains.)
26. B. (A gray circle is successively added.)

27. 46. (The series always increases by 6.)
28. A and C, myrtle and thyme, respectively. (Both are herbs.)
29. 307. (It's the difference between the first and third numbers.)
30. A; blizzard. (This is not a wind.)
31. 14. (The series alternately subtracts 2 and adds 5.)
32. 2. (Calculate the difference between the sum of the numbers in the upper circles and the sum of the numbers in the lower circles.)
33. D. (The second figure in each series adds a similar gray shape with a solid line around it.)
34. B. (The interior of the figure becomes 3 lines: thin, thick, and thin.)
35. A and C, rest and refreshed. (These are both synonyms for relax.)
36. 3. (Divide the first number by the third number.)
37. B; handlebars.
38. 0.05, 0.2, 3/8 (0.375), 2/5 (0.4), 8/10 (0.8).
39. Husband.
40. 10. (The series alternates by adding 3 and subtracting 2.)
41. D; Steven. (This is a man's name; Frances, Jenna, Laura, and Maria are women's names.)
42. 8. (Divide the second number by the first number.)
43. D. (The figure is reversed.)
44. 31. (The series alternates by adding 3 and subtracting 1.)
45. 9. (Calculate the difference between the first and third numbers.)
46. 30. (Calculate the sum of the first and second numbers, the second and the third, the third and the fourth, etc.)
47. D; Rumpelstiltskin. (He is a male character; Thumbelina, Rapunzel, Cinderella, and Goldilocks are all female characters.)
48. 19. (There are two alternating series; the first increases by 4 and the second by 5.)
49. 24. (Calculate the product of the numbers of the triangle.)
50. F. (The gray figure alternates with the white figure.)

Test 5

1. What is the missing word?

Book:library::bottle of wine:…

A. vineyard
B. distillery
C. antique dealer
D. wine cellar
E. liquor

2. Find the missing number.

13   10   15   13   17   16   …

3. Unscramble the following letters to find the word that is not a planet.

A. rmuycre
B. surnat
C. tulop
D. aarcatcnit
E. nesuv

4. Find the missing number.

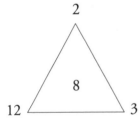 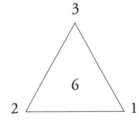 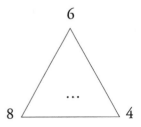

5. Find the missing number.

3   9   27   ...   243   729

6. Find the missing number.

1	20
6	8

12	15
5	3

18	4
9	...

7. Complete the series with the correct name.

Esmeralda
Aurora
Mowgli
Gaston
...
A. Linus   B. Ursula   C. Anastasia   D. Elroy   E. Daphne

8. Find the missing number.

20   (110)   35
11   (   )   23

9. Which figure does not belong?

A   B   C   D   E

10. Find the missing number.

4   7   11   18   ...   47   76   123

11. Which word does not belong?

A. expectant
B. parturient
C. excellent
D. pregnant
E. gravid

12. Find the missing number.

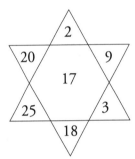 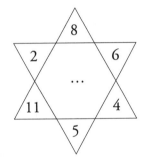

13. Choose the correct response.

Some insects don't fly.

A. definitely true
B. not true
C. sometimes true
D. an opinion

14. Find the missing number.

8   10   12

4   15   ...

10   14   18

15. Insert the correct figure.

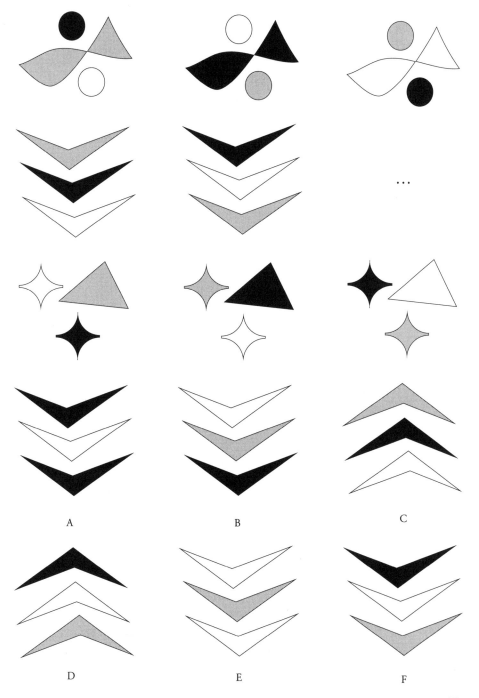

16. What is the missing number?

343:7::1,331:...

A. 13   B. 9   C. 10   D. 1,000   E. 11

17. Which word does not belong?

A.   Superior
B.   Titicaca
C.   Huron
D.   Volga
E.   Victoria

18. Find the missing number.

10-15-7   17-12-3   20-9-...

19. Find the missing letter.

A-J-D   F-F-C   H-B-...

20. Find the missing numbers.

8   1   12   6   20   16

21. Which figure does not belong?

A   B   C   D   E

22. Find the word that means the same thing as each of the other two.

Misshapen (....) Perverse

23. What is the next figure in the series?

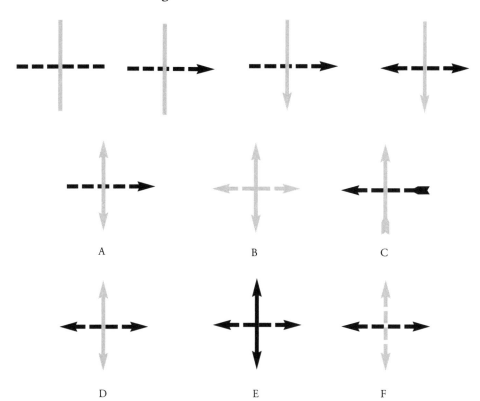

A   B   C

D   E   F

24. Find the missing number.

12   3   10   6   8   9   6   12   ...

25. Unscramble the following letters to find the animal that is not a bird.

    A.   ulrtevu
    B.   nnuegip
    C.   torosre
    D.   arbe
    E.   ngipeo

26. Find the missing number.

17   28   39   50   61   72   ...

27. Which word is not a synonym of the others?

A.   poster
B.   sign
C.   insert
D.   placard
E.   flyer

28. Find the missing number.

23   (13)   10

60   ( )   21

29. Which two words are similar?

A. tangle   B. thorn   C. intersection   D. uproar   E. snarl

30. Find the missing number.

18   20   19   21   20   22   21   ...

31. Find the missing number.

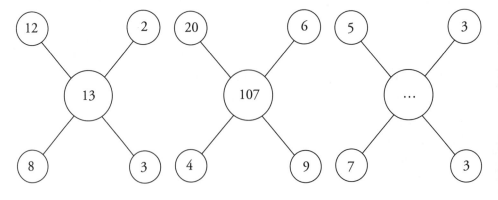

32. Which figure does not belong?

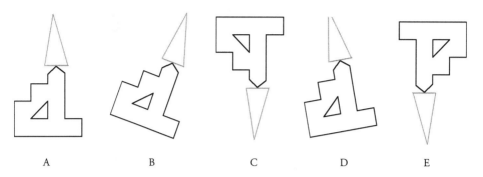

A   B   C   D   E

33. Find the word that means the same thing as each of the other two.

Creased (....) Bankrupt

34. Choose the correct response.

A rainbow contains 8 colors.

A.   definitely true
B.   not true
C.   sometimes true
D.   an opinion

35. Complete the series with the correct number.

3
5
7
11
...
A. 15   B. 20   C. 13   D. 12   E. 18

36. Find the missing letter.

J   L   N   P   R   ...

37. What is the missing figure?

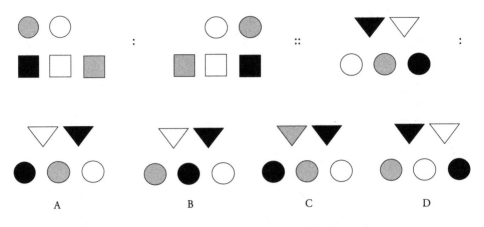

A   B   C   D

38. What is the missing number?

2:8::3:...

A. 15   B. 1   C. 10   D. 27   E. 9

39. Find the missing letter.

A   E   I   M   ...

40. Find the missing number.

1   4   2   8   4   16   ...

41. Find the missing letter.

B:Y::E:...

A.   G
B.   V
C.   Z
D.   M
E.   S

42. Insert the correct figure.

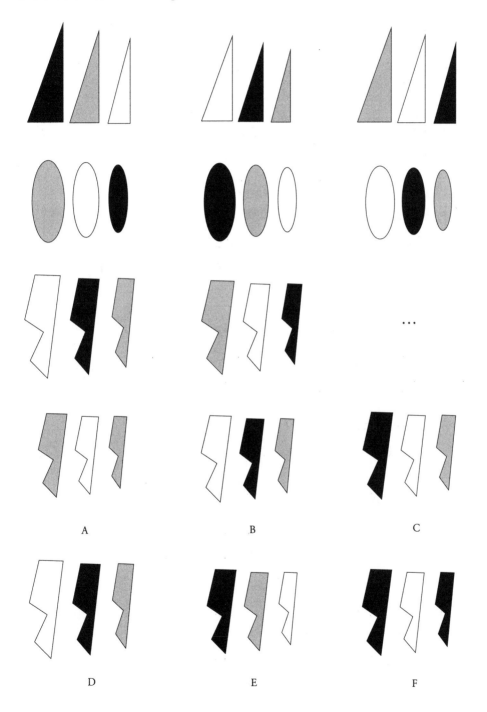

A

B

C

D

E

F

43. Find the missing number.

8	65	8
6	...	7
12	13	1

44. Find the missing number.

68   84   62   81   56   78   50...

45. Which number does not belong?

13   23   19   3   1   18

46. Unscramble the following letters to find the word that is not a profession.

A.   tnirepa
B.   dutnest
C.   rtcarotnoc
D.   reyalw
E.   cortdo

47. Rearrange the numbers from smallest to largest.

0.4   1/10   7/4   0.08   0.9

48. Find the missing number.

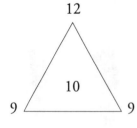 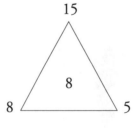 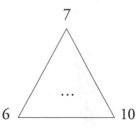

49. What is the next figure in the series?

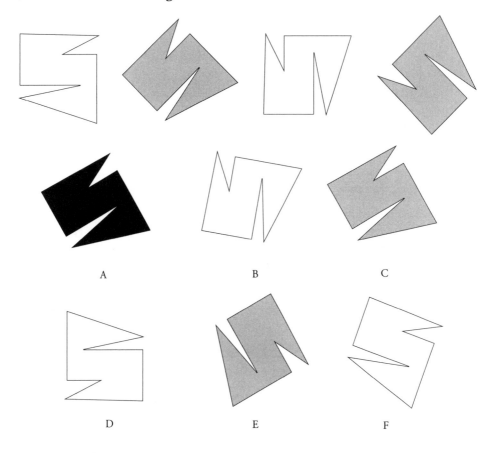

A	B	C
D	E	F

50. Unscramble the following letters to find the word that is not a number.

A. rtneehit
B. eninewtytn
C. tehplaba
D. vifrihytte
E. orfyt

Answers

1. D; wine cellar.
2. 19. (There are two alternating series; the first increases by 2 and the second by 3.)
3. D; Antarctica. (This is a continent; Mercury, Saturn, Pluto, and Venus are planets.)
4. 12. (Divide the numbers at the base of the triangles and multiply by the number at the vertex.)
5. 81. (The series increases by multiples of 3.)
6. 4. (The sum of the numbers in the square is always 35.)
7. B; Ursula. (They are all Walt Disney characters.)
8. 68. (Calculate the sum of the outer numbers and multiply the result by 2.)
9. D. (The figure is reversed.)
10. 29. (Add the first number to the second number, the second number to the third number, etc.)
11. C; excellent.
12. 10. (Calculate the difference between the sum of the numbers in the two large triangles that form each star.)
13. A.
14. 26. (Calculate the sum of the outer numbers and divide the result by 2.)
15. B. (The series alternates white, black, and gray in each component.)
16. E; 11. (It's the cube root.)
17. D; Volga. (It's a river, not a lake.)
18. 3. (The sum of each series is always 32.)
19. E. (The sum of the numerical equivalents of the letters in each series is 15.)
20. 16 and 11. (There are two alternating series; the first increases by 4 and the second by 5.)
21. C. (The figure is reversed.)
22. Twisted.
23. D. (Each figure adds another arrow.)
24. 4. (There are two alternating series; the first decreases by 2 and the second increases by 3.)

25. D; bear. (This is a mammal; vulture, penguin, rooster, and pigeon are birds.)
26. 83. (The series always increases by 11.)
27. C; insert.
28. 39. (Calculate the difference between the first and third number.)
29. A and E, tangle and snarl, respectively.
30. 23. (The series alternately adds 2 and subtracts 1.)
31. 5. (Calculate the product of the numbers in the upper circles and subtract the sum of the numbers in the lower circles.)
32. C. (The figure is reversed.)
33. Folded.
34. B.
35. C; 13. (They are all prime numbers.)
36. T. (The series always skips a letter.)
37. A. (The figure is reversed.)
38. D; 27. (It's the cube.)
39. Q. (The series always skips three letters.)
40. 8. (The series alternately multiplies by 4 and divides by 2.)
41. B; V. (B is the second letter from the beginning of the alphabet and Y is the second from the end; E is the fifth letter from the beginning and V is the fifth from the end.)
42. E. (The series alternates white, black, and gray in the components of the figure.)
43. 43. (Calculate the product of the outer numbers and add 1.)
44. 75. (There are two alternating series; the first decreases by 6 and the second by 3.)
45. 18. (It's the only even number.)
46. B; student. (This is not a profession; painter, contractor, lawyer, and doctor are professions.)
47. 0.08, 1/10 (0.1), 0.4, 0.9, 7/4 (1.75).
48. 3. (The difference between the outer and inner numbers is always 20.)
49. D. (The figure rotates 45 degrees counterclockwise and alternates between gray, white, and gray.)
50. C; alphabet. (The numbers are thirteen, twenty-nine, thirty-five, and forty.)

Test 6

1. Find the missing number.

9   22   35   48   61   74   ...

2. Which two words are similar?

A. go   B. always   C. rejoice   D. Frances   E. tasty

3. Find the missing number.

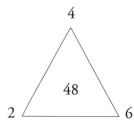
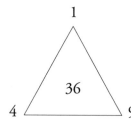
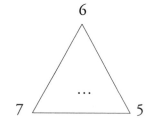

4. Unscramble the following letters to find the word that is not a country.

    A.   gtulpora
    B.   hgnatasafni
    C.   rebnil
    D.   raguhny
    E.   danaca

5. Find the missing numbers.

5   1   13   10   29   28

6. Find the missing number.

30	4
5	8

41	1
18	9

28	3
7	...

7. Complete the series with the correct city.

Berlin
Prague
Beijing
London
...

A. Barcelona   B. Rome   C. New York   D. Bombay   E. Nice

8. Find the missing number.

2   6   18   54   162   ...

9. Which term is the most appropriate?

To diminish both sensory awareness and motor response.

A. paralyze   B. numb   C. stiffen

10. Which figure does not belong?

A   B   C   D   E

11. Which word is not a synonym of the others?

A. lacerate
B. scratch
C. scrape
D. tear
E. cut

12. Find the missing number.

10   6   15   5   20   4   ...

13. Find the word that means the same thing as each of the other two.

Intelligent (....) Vibrant

14. Find the missing number.

8-9-2   12-7-4   21-4-...

15. Find the missing number.

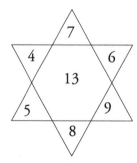 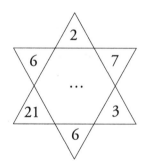

16. What is the missing word?

31:January::28:...

A. February B. March C. days D. month E. April

17. Insert the correct figure.

A

B

C

D

E

F

18. Which figure does not belong?

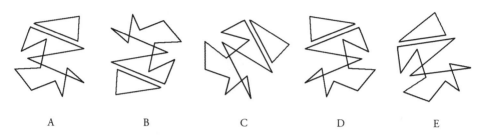

A   B   C   D   E

19. Which title does not belong?

A. Twelfth Night
B. The Taming of the Shrew
C. The Merchant of Venice
D. The Jew of Malta
E. Titus Andronicus

20. Find the missing number.

2   5   11   23   47   ...

21. Which name does not belong?

A. Beethoven   B. Pavarotti   C. Chopin   D. Handel   E. Mozart

22. What is the missing number?

4:3::12:...

A. 24   B. 9   C. 6   D. 8   E. 4

23. Find the missing letter.

C-E-J   F-F-F   C-F-...

24. Find the missing number.

10   8   13   11   16   14   ...

25. **What is the missing word?**

Yes:English::Si:...

A. French
B. Dutch
C. Italian
D. Latin
E. Polish

26. **Find the missing number.**

6   (7)   8

9   ( )   3

27. **What is the next figure in the series?**

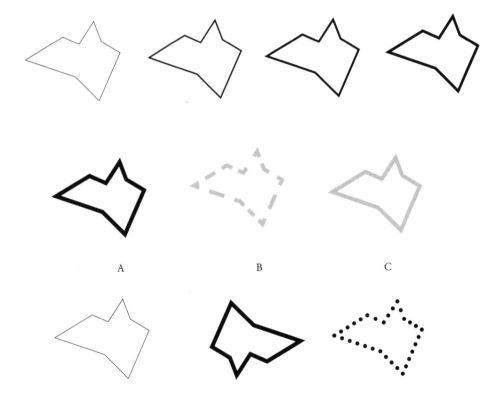

A   B   C

D   E   F

28. Find the missing number.

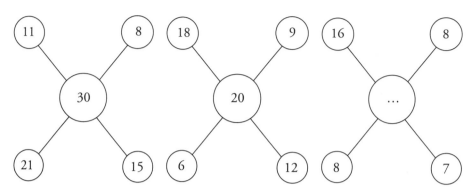

29. Which two words are similar?

A. beret   B. glasses   C. earrings   D. bowler   E. gloves

30. Find the missing number.

5	3	4
4	6	...
7	9	8

31. Rearrange the numbers from smallest to largest.

2.3   4/3   1/5   0.01   0.6

32. Unscramble the following letters to find the word that is not a sea.

A.   talcib
B.   henrytnari
C.   edr
D.   isrepan
E.   retrnemeidaan

33. Find the missing number.

3   10   9   16   15   22   ...

34. What is the missing word?

Big:small::black:...

A. gray
B. white
C. discolored
D. clear
E. opaque

35. Find the missing number.

2   1   2   2   3   4   ...

36. What is the missing word?

Wordsworth:poem::Puccini:...

A. sounds
B. opera
C. concert
D. notes
E. symphony

37. Which figure does not belong?

A   B   C   D   E

38. What is the missing figure?

 : :: :

A B C D

39. Which two words are similar?

A. recurring   B. fast   C. continual   D. orderly   E. occasional

40. Find the missing number.

10	12	22
18	23	41
32	...	83

41. Unscramble the following letters to find the word that is not a flower.

A. ormserip
B. atnnoraci
C. loveti
D. ebehc
E. itpul

42. What is the next figure in the series?

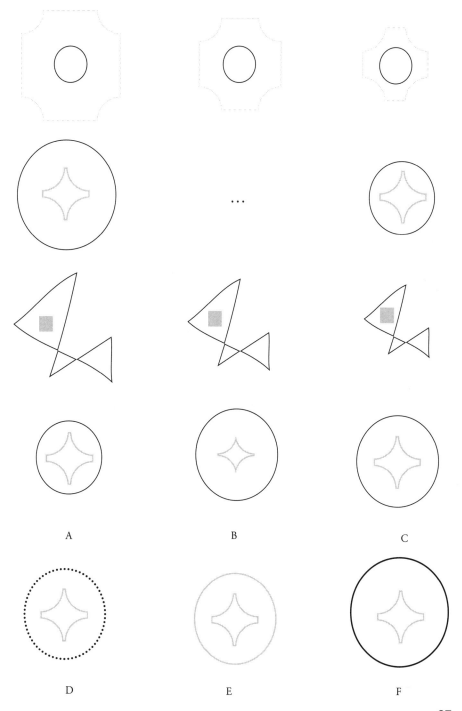

A

B

C

D

E

F

43. What is the missing number?

4:16::3:...

A. 6
B. 9
C. 12
D. 27
E. 30

44. Find the missing number.

10	7	3
22	...	8
13	2	11

45. Complete the series with the correct word.

Cycling
Roller skating
Race car driving
In-line skating
...

A. soccer   B. basketball   C. motorcycling   D. poker   E. baseball

46. Find the missing number.

| 13 | 10 | 17 | 15 | 21 | ... | 25 | 25 |

47. Find the missing number.

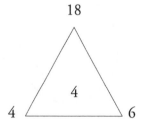 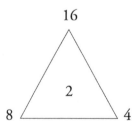 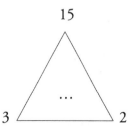

48. What is the next figure in the series?

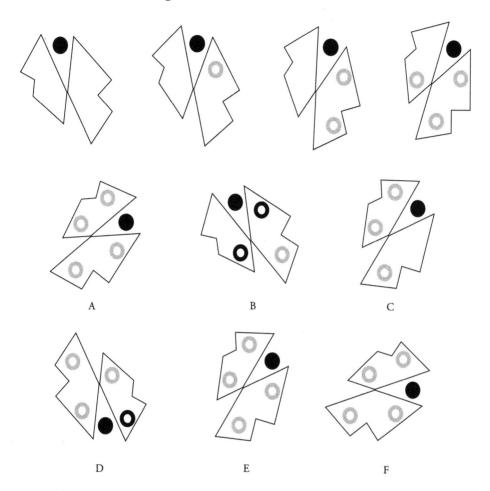

A   B   C

D   E   F

49. Find the missing number.

  4   9   16   25   ...   49   64

50. Find the missing letter.

  B   D   F   H   J   ...

Answers

1. 87. (The series increases by 13.)
2. A and C, go and rejoice, respectively. (Both are verbs.)
3. 210. (Multiply the outer numbers.)
4. C; Berlin. (This is a city; Portugal, Afghanistan, Hungary, and Canada are countries.)
5. 21 and 19. (There are two alternate series; the first increases by 8 and the second by 9.)
6. 5. (The largest number minus the other three numbers in each square is equal to 13.)
7. B; Rome. (They are all capital cities.)
8. 486. (The series increases by multiples of 3.)
9. B; numb.
10. C. (The figure is reversed.)
11. D; tear.
12. 25. (There are two alternating series; the first increases by 5 and the second decreases by 1.)
13. Bright.
14. 10. (Subtract the third number from the sum of the first two; the answer is always 15.)
15. 15. (Calculate the sum of the numbers in the outer triangles and divide the result by 3.)
16. A; February.
17. B. (Each series alternates between white, black, and gray, and the figure rotates counterclockwise.)
18. D. (The figure is reversed.)
19. D; The Jew of Malta. (This was written by Christopher Marlowe; the others were all written by Shakespeare.)
20. 95. (Double each number and add 1.)
21. B; Pavarotti. (He is a singer, not a composer.)
22. B; 9. (Multiply the first number by ¾.)
23. I. (The sum of the numerical equivalents of the letters in each series is always 18.)
24. 19. (The series alternately subtracts 2 and adds 5.)
25. C; Italian.

26. 6. (Calculate the sum of the outer numbers and divide the result by 2.)
27. A. (The width of the figure's outline progressively increases.)
28. 14. (The difference between the sum of the outer numbers and the inner number is always 25.)
29. A and D, beret and bowler, respectively. (These are two types of hats.)
30. 5. (Calculate the sum of the first and second number and divide the result by 2.)
31. 0.01, 1/5(0.2), 0.6, 4/3(1.33), 2.3.
32. D; Persian. (This is a gulf; Baltic, Tyrrhenian, Red, and Mediterranean are seas.)
33. 21. (The series alternately adds 7 and subtracts 1.)
34. B; white.
35. 6. (Calculate the sum of the first and second number, the second and the third, etc., and subtract 1.)
36. B; opera.
37. D. (The figure is reversed.)
38. B. (The figure is reversed and rotates 90 degrees counterclockwise.)
39. A and C, recurring and continual, respectively. (They are synonyms of frequent.)
40. 51. (It's the difference between the first and third numbers.)
41. D; beech. (This is a tree; primrose, carnation, violet, and tulip are flowers.)
42. C. (The size of the outer figure progressively decreases.)
43. B; 9.
44. 14. (Calculate the difference between the outer numbers.)
45. C; motorcycling. (They are all sports involving wheels.)
46. 20. (There are two alternating series; the first increases by 4 and the second by 5.)
47. 5. (Subtract the numbers at the base of the triangle from the number at the vertex and divide the result by 2.)
48. E. (The figure rotates 15 degrees clockwise and successively adds a gray circle.)
49. 36. (The numbers are the squares of 2, 3, 4, 5, etc.)
50. L. (The series always skips a letter.)

Test 7

1. Unscramble the following letters to find the word that is not an American city.

   A. noobst
   B. drolnao
   C. cgihoca
   D. lobaceran
   E. rmateconas

2. Find the missing number.

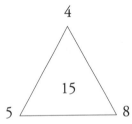
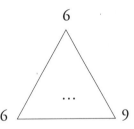

3. Choose the correct response.

   All rivers flow into the sea.

   A. definitely true
   B. not true
   C. sometimes true
   D. an opinion

4. Find the missing number.

   2   8   14   20   ...   32

5. Which figure does not belong?

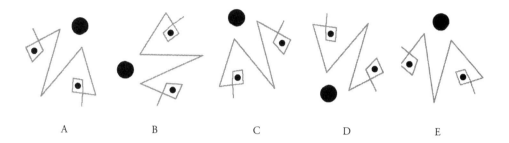

A   B   C   D   E

6. Complete the series with the correct word.

Tsunami
Earthquake
Landslide
Tornado
...

A. cloud   B. mountain   C. hurricane   D. thunder   E. lightning

7. Find the missing numbers.

4   7   6   10   10   16

8. Find the missing letter.

E-A-D   A-A-H   C-C-...

9. Find the missing number.

3	12
6	9

8	11
7	4

10	1
5	...

10. Find the missing number.

95   98   89   95   83   ...   77   89

11. Which word is not a synonym of the others?

    A.   change
    B.   metamorphosis
    C.   transformation
    D.   disguise
    E.   mutation

12. Find the missing number.

6   15   24   33   42   ...

13. Which definition is the most appropriate?

To annul a law, a decree, etc., by means of a public act.

A. to renounce   B. to abolish   C. to revoke

14. Find the missing number.

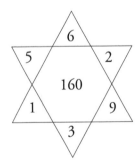 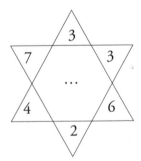

15. Find the word that means the same thing as each of the other two.

Peel (....) Pelt

16. Insert the correct figure.

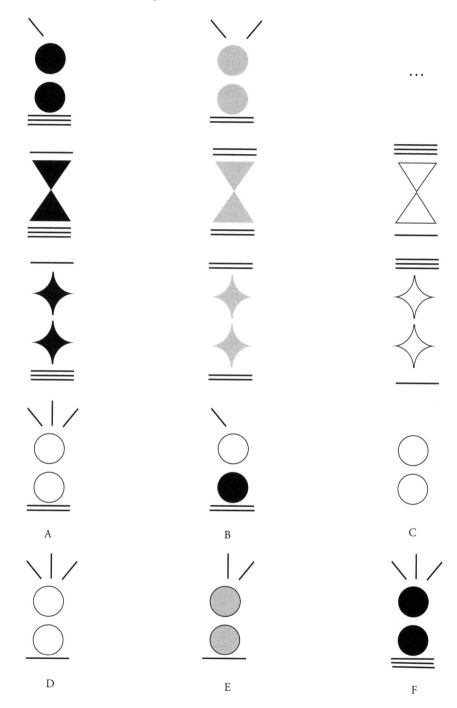

17. Which figure does not belong?

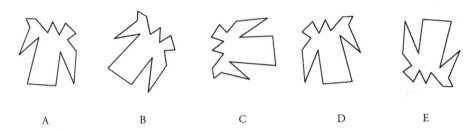

A   B   C   D   E

18. Find the missing number.

10-4-5   17-8-8   14-6-...

19. What is the missing name?

battery:Volta::radio:...

A. Marconi   B. Edison   C. Galilei   D. Bell   E. Newton

20. Find the missing number.

3   8   18   38   ...   158   318

21. Unscramble the following letters to find the name that is not a U.S. President.

A.   shoreienwe
B.   chirullch
C.   delveclan
D.   stanginhow
E.   fonjerfes

22. Find the missing number.

564   (4)   254
841   ( )   511

23. Find the word that means the same thing as each of the other two.

Control (....) Average

24. Find the missing number.

9	7	5
7	8	...
4	3	14

25. What is the next figure in the series?

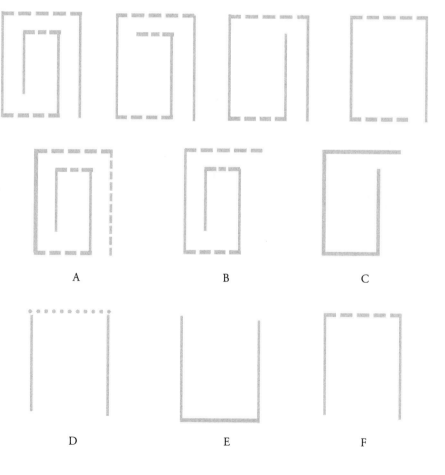

A   B   C

D   E   F

26. Find the missing letter.

   N   L   J   H   F   ...

27. Find the missing number.

   31   29   23   19   ...   13   11   7

28. Which word is not a synonym of the others?

   A.   arise
   B.   appear
   C.   originate
   D.   show
   E.   spring

29. Find the missing number.

   9   (27)   9

   3   ( )   8

30. Find the word that means the same thing as each of the other two.

   Ground-breaking (....) Freedom-fighter

31. Find the missing number.

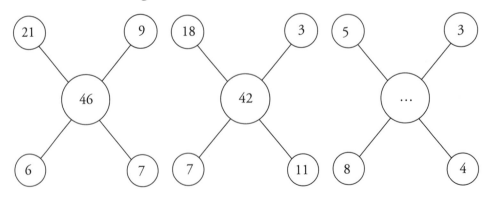

32. Which figure does not belong?

A   B   C   D   E

33. Which city does not belong?

A. Beijing
B. Bogota
C. Berlin
D. Baltimore
E. Budapest

34. Find the missing number.

7   2   15   11   23   ...

35. Complete the series with the correct word.

Tempera
Watercolors
Pens
Crayons
...
A. clay   B. ceramic   C. pencils   D. paper   E. chisel

36. Rearrange the numbers from smallest to largest.

0.4   9/5   1/20   0.08   3.5

37. What is the missing figure?

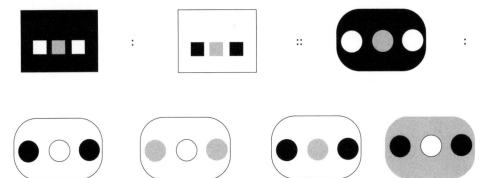

A	B	C	D

38. Unscramble the following letters to find the word that is not a fish.

- A. rutot
- B. prca
- C. dota
- D. dulnefro
- E. noslam

39. What is the missing word?

Ball:soccer::foil:…

- A. wrestling
- B. fencing
- C. darts
- D. archery
- E. tennis

40. What is the missing word?

7:week::365:…

A. day   B. shiny   C. year   D. century   E. month

41. Insert the correct figure.

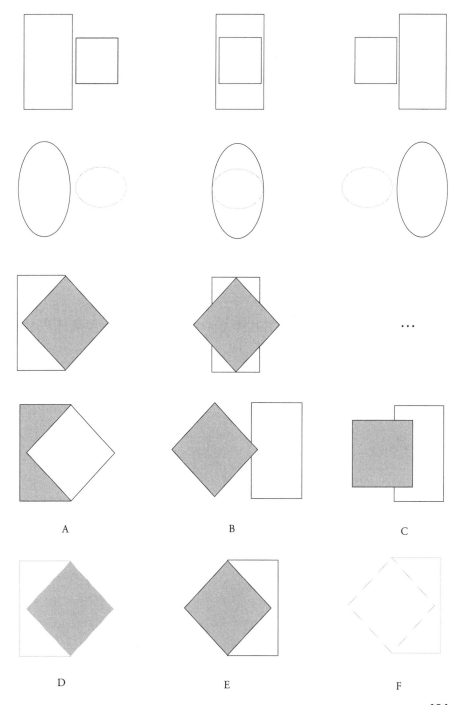

A

B

C

D

E

F

42. Find the missing number.

25	6	19
31	...	21
8	2	6

43. Find the missing letter.

C   F   I   L   ...

44. Which name does not belong?

A.   Socrates
B.   Plato
C.   Seneca
D.   Virgil
E.   Aristotle

45. Unscramble the following letters to find the word that is not a lake.

A.   nctagmhi
B.   heoat
C.   tarrce
D.   hpilncmaa
E.   sdohun

46. Find the missing number.

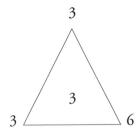 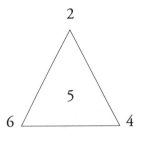 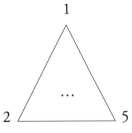

47. What is the next figure in the series?

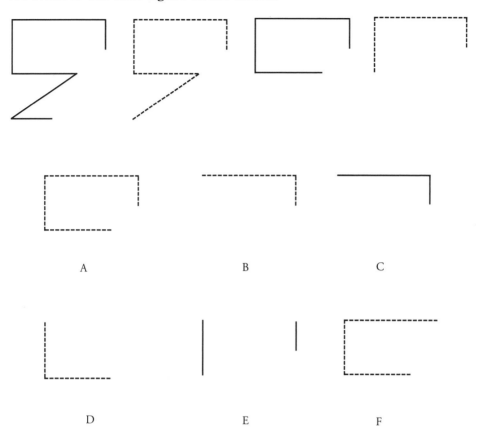

A   B   C

D   E   F

48. Find the missing number.

1   2   3   7   22   ...

49. Find the missing number.

18   21   14   17   ...   13   6   9   2

50. Find the word that means the same thing as each of the other two.

Observe (....) Tone

Answers

1. D; Barcelona. (This is a Spanish city; Boston, Orlando, Chicago, and Sacramento are American cities.)
2. 11. (The sum of the outer numbers added to the inner number is always 32.)
3. B.
4. 26. (The series increases by 6.)
5. C. (The figure is reversed.)
6. C; hurricane. (They are all natural disasters.)
7. 8 and 13. (There are two alternating series; the first increases by 2 and the second by 3.)
8. D. (The sum of the numerical equivalents of the letters in each series is always 10.)
9. 14. (The sum of the numbers in each square is always 30.)
10. 92. (There are two alternating series; the first decreases by 6 and the second by 3.)
11. D; disguise.
12. 51. (The series increases by 9.)
13. C; to revoke.
14. 156. (Multiply the sum of the numbers in the first large triangle by the sum of the numbers in the second.)
15. Skin.
16. D. (The lower lines decrease in number, the upper lines increase, and the colors alternate between white, black, and gray.)
17. D. (The figure is reversed.)
18. 7. (The first number minus the sum of the last two numbers is always 1.)
19. A; Marconi.
20. 78. (Add 1 to the previous number and multiply by 2.)
21. B; Churchill. (He was a British prime minister; Eisenhower, Cleveland, Washington, and Jefferson were U.S. presidents.)
22. 6. (Calculate the difference between the sum of the digits of the first number and the sum of the digits of the third number.)
23. Moderate.
24. 6. (The sum of the numbers is always 21.)

25. F. (Each figure in the series progressively loses a line.)
26. D. (The series skips one letter in reverse alphabetical order.)
27. 17. (The series is comprised of prime numbers in descending order.)
28. D; show.
29. 8. (Multiply the outer numbers and divide the result by 3.)
30. Revolutionary.
31. 23. (The inner number minus the sum of the outer numbers is always 3.)
32. C. (The figure is reversed.)
33. D; Baltimore. (This is a U.S. city; the others are all country capitals.)
34. 20. (There are two alternating series; the first increases by 8 and the second by 9.)
35. C; pencils. (They are all tools for coloring.)
36. 1/20 (0.05), 0.08, 0.4, 9/5 (1.8), 3.5.
37. C. (The white becomes black and vice versa.)
38. C; toad. (This is an amphibian; trout, carp, flounder, and salmon are types of fish.)
39. B; fencing.
40. C; year.
41. E. (The superimposed figure moves progressively to the left.)
42. 10. (The third number is the difference between the first and second numbers.)
43. O. (The series always skips 2 letters.)
44. D; Virgil. (He was a poet, not a philosopher.)
45. E; Hudson. (This is a river; Michigan, Tahoe, Crater, and Champlain are all lakes.)
46. 7. (Calculate the sum of the numbers in the lower angles and divide by the corresponding number in the upper angle.)
47. C. (The figure successively loses a segment and alternates between solid and broken lines.)
48. 155. (Multiply the first number by the second number, the second by the third, etc., and add 1.)
49. 10. (The series alternately adds 3 and subtracts 7.)
50. Note.

Test 8

1. What is the missing location?

Nepal:Asia::Congo:...

A. Africa
B. Central America
C. Zaire
D. Namibia
E. Australia

2. Find the missing number.

7   7   6   10   5   13   4   ...

3. Unscramble the following letters to find the word that is not a feline.

A. napreth
B. onil
C. agaruj
D. pedralo
E. rutlet

4. Find the missing number.

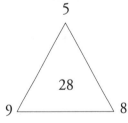
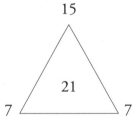
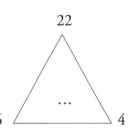

5. Find the missing number.

  2   5   14   ...   122

6. Find the word that means the same thing as each of the other two.

  Option (....) Quality

7. Find the missing number.

7	8
5	10

2	6
4	4

12	4
6	...

8. Choose the correct response.

  If a triangle does not have two or three equal sides it is scalene.

  A.   definitely true
  B.   not true
  C.   sometimes true
  D.   an opinion

9. Find the missing number.

  12   11   16   16   20   ...   24   26

10. Complete the series with the correct word.

  abacus
  baby
  chariot
  dart
  ...
  A. marine   B. crossbow   C. hermit   D. jaguar   E. eggplant

11. Which figure does not belong?

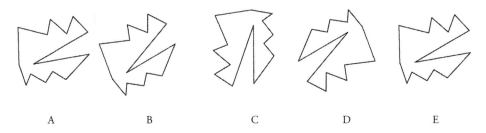

A   B   C   D   E

12. Which word is not a synonym of the others?

A. precise
B. exact
C. particular
D. local
E. specific

13. Find the missing number.

15   17   16   18   17   ...

14. Which term is the most appropriate?

A collection of data and documents on a certain topic.

A. article   B. review   C. dossier

15. Find the missing number.

411   (1)   212
131   ( )   111

16. Find the word that means the same thing as each of the other two.

Mail (....) Assignment

17. Insert the correct figure.

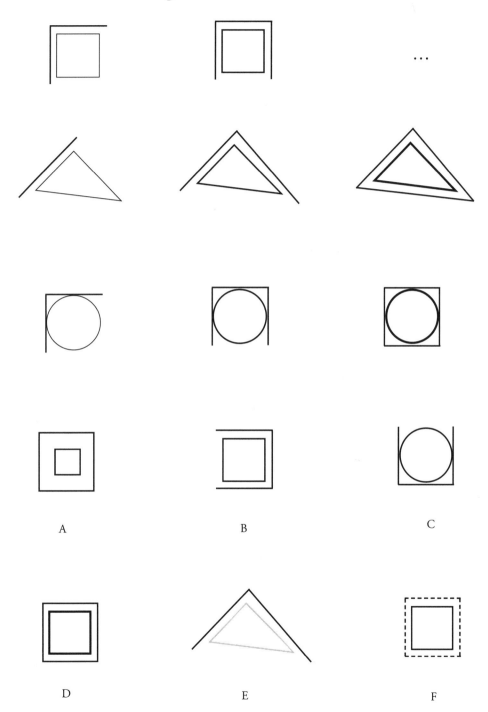

A

B

C

D

E

F

18. Find the missing number.

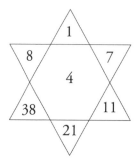 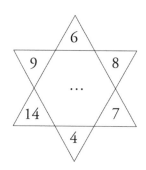

19. What is the missing name?

telephone:Bell::lightbulb:...

A. Newton
B. Edison
C. Fermi
D. Pasteur
E. Sabin

20. Find the word that means the same thing as each of the other two.

Write (....) Enclosure

21. Which figure does not belong?

    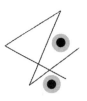

A   B   C   D   E

22. What is the next figure in the series?

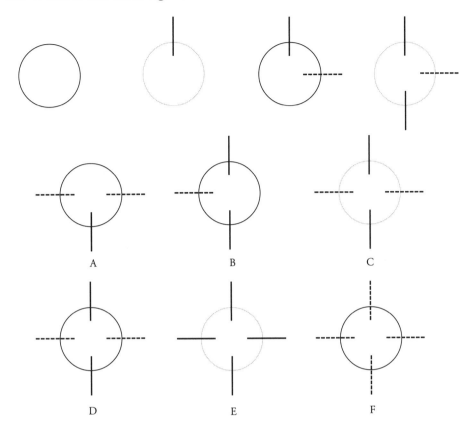

A   B   C

D   E   F

23. Find the missing number.

77   85   93   101   109   117   ...

24. Which lake does not belong?

A. Huron
B. Erie
C. Superior
D. Victoria
E. Ontario

25. Find the missing number.

50   (149)   3

11   (   )   9

26. Complete the series with the correct state.

Georgia
Virginia
Maine
New York
...

A. Oregon   B. Massachusetts   C. Colorado   D. Nevada   E. Texas

27. Find the missing number.

7-10-3   6-12-2   9-7-...

28. Find the missing number.

8   11   10   8   12   5   14   ...

29. Which number does not belong?

35   17   44   62   80   11

30. Find the missing number.

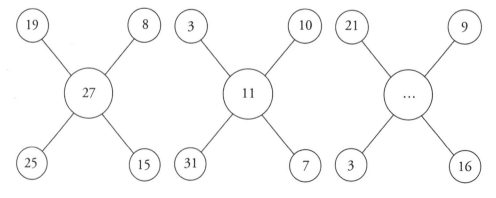

31. Which figure does not belong?

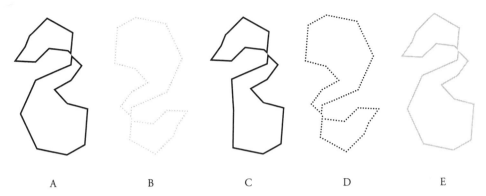

A   B   C   D   E

32. Find the missing letter.

R-O-M   S-U-F   G-...-Y

33. Find the missing number.

5	4	4
8	6	...
10	10	5

34. Find the word that means the same thing as each of the other two.

Sidewalk (....) Restrain

35. Which word is not a synonym of the others?

A. carbonated
B. effervescent
C. bubbly
D. varnished
E. fizzy

36. What is the missing figure?

 : ::  :

A   B   C   D

37. Find the missing number.

5	39	8
7	...	3
4	23	6

38. Find the word that means the same thing as each of the other two.

Resonance (....) Sane

39. Find the missing number.

5   6   8   11   15   ...

40. Find the missing letter.

K   M   O   Q   S   ...

41. Find the missing number.

8   8   7   10   6   ...

42. Insert the missing figure.

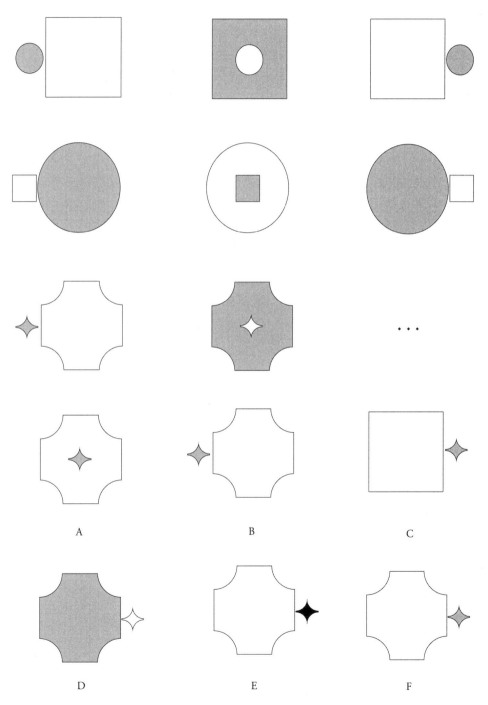

43. Find the missing number.

7   10   8   11   9   ...

44. Unscramble the following letters to find the city that is not a state capital.

  A. noluhoul
  B. flipsdringe
  C. lasald
  D. clinlon
  E. greahil

45. Rearrange the numbers from smallest to largest.

0.4   3/90   21/3   0.02   2.5

46. What is the missing word?

Paintbrush:artist::scalpel:...

  A. clerk
  B. surgeon
  C. house painter
  D. nutritionist
  E. homeopath

47. Find the missing number.

575   287   143   71   ...   17

48. Find the missing number.

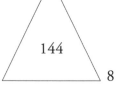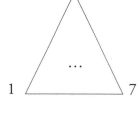

49. What is the next figure in the series?

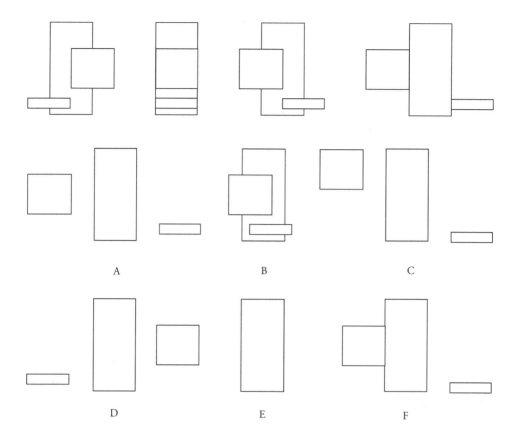

A

B

C

D

E

F

50. Unscramble the following letters to find the word that is not a state.

- A. besakrna
- B. dlecelanv
- C. tnaoman
- D. facanoirli
- E. nynsvapaline

Answers

1. A; Africa.
2. 16. (There are two alternating series; the first decreases by 1 and the second increases by 3.)
3. E; turtle. (This is a reptile; panther, lion, jaguar, and leopard are felines.)
4. 18. (The sum of the outer and inner numbers of the triangle is always 50.)
5. 41. (Multiply each number in the series by 3 and subtract 1.)
6. Choice.
7. 10. (The sum of the upper numbers is equal to the sum of the lower numbers.)
8. A.
9. 21. (There are two alternating series; the first increases by 4 and the second by 5.)
10. E; eggplant. (The sequence is in alphabetical order.)
11. C. (The figure is reversed.)
12. D; local.
13. 19. (The series alternately adds 2 and subtracts 1.)
14. C; dossier.
15. 2. (Calculate the difference between the sums of the individual digits of the outer numbers.)
16. Post.
17. D. (The outer figure progressively gains sides and the inner shape's outline thickens.)
18. 42. (The sum of the numbers in each star is 90.)
19. B; Edison.
20. Pen.
21. C. (The figure is reversed.)
22. D. (The lines progressively increase in number and the circles alternate between black and gray.)
23. 125. (The series progressively increases by 8.)
24. D; Victoria. (The others are all Great Lakes.)
25. 98. (Multiply the first number by the third number and subtract 1.)
26. B; Massachusetts. (They are all states in the eastern U.S.)

27. 4. (The sum of each series is always 20.)
28. 2. (There are two alternating series; the first increases by 2 and the second decreases by 3.)
29. 11. (The sum of the single digits in each number is always 8.)
30. 9. (The difference between the outer numbers and the inner number is always 40.)
31. C. (The figure is a different shape.)
32. N. (The sum of the numerical equivalents of each series of letters is 46.)
33. 3. (The difference between the sum of the outer numbers and the inner numbers is always 5.)
34. Curb.
35. D; varnished.
36. B. (The black becomes gray and vice versa, and the solid line on the outside becomes broken.)
37. 20. (Multiply the first number in the row by the third number and subtract 1.)
38. Sound.
39. 20. (The series increases by adding 1, 2, 3, etc., to the previous number.)
40. U. (The series always skips a letter.)
41. 12. (There are two alternating series; the first decreases by 1 and the second increases by 2.)
42. F. (In each figure, the shape on the left moves to the right and the two shapes alternate white and gray.)
43. 12. (The series alternately adds 3 and subtracts 2.)
44. C; Dallas. (This is a city; Honolulu, Springfield, Lincoln, and Raleigh are state capitals.)
45. 0.02, 3/90 (0.03), 0.4, 2.5, 21/3 (7).
46. B; surgeon.
47. 35. (For each number in the series, subtract 1 and divide by 2.)
48. 63. (Calculate the product of the outer numbers.)
49. A. (The two shapes on top of the rectangle progressively move left and right.)
50. B; Cleveland. (This is a city; Nebraska, Montana, California, and Pennsylvania are states.)

Part 2

Measuring Your Specific Abilities

Numerical Test

1. Find the missing number.

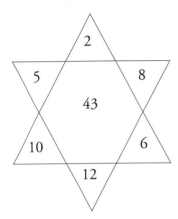 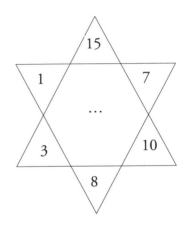

2. Find the missing number.

15   18   16   19   17   ...

3. Find the missing number.

400   (2)   396

112   ( )   98

4. Find the missing number.

8   1   10   4   12   7   14   ...

5. Find the missing number.

1   4   5   9   14   ...   37   60

6. Find the missing numbers.

13   (29)   16
44   ( )   31

6   (6)   2
4   (6)   3
2   ( )   9

7. What is the missing number?

5:25::6:...

A. 60   B. 22   C. 54   D. 38   E. 36

8. Find the missing number.

1   1   2   3   7   ...

9. Find the missing number.

9	12	16	11
8	10	...	9
3	18	9	18
13	12	17	6

10. Find the missing number.

11. Find the missing numbers.

6	5	5	7	4	...	3	11
1	3	3	5	7	...	17	27

12. Find the missing number.

5	9	14
4	8	12
1	3	...

13. Find the missing number.

12	(60)	10
3	( )	18

14. Find the missing number.

21	9
17	13

14	2
10	6

27	15
23	...

15. Find the missing numbers.

36   43   50   57   78   85

16. Find the missing number.

13   10   19   13   25   16   ...

17. Find the missing number.

8   7   6

1   9   11

2   10   ...

18. Find the missing number.

 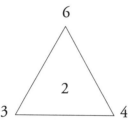 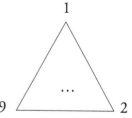

19. Find the missing numbers.

10   8   8   5   4   -1

20. Find the missing number.

9   11   20   31   51   ...

21. Find the missing number.

2   2   5

6   8   ...

7   1   8

22. Find the missing number.

5   4   7   3   9   2   11   ...

23. Find the missing number.

8	0	8
7	6	...
2	9	5

24. Find the missing numbers.

6   11   15   19   33   35

25. What is the missing number?

12:6::44:...

A. 10   B. 28   C. 22   D. 20   E. 60

26. Find the missing number.

4	4	3	1
2	4	...	6
3	1	1	2
1	1	3	1

27. Find the missing number.

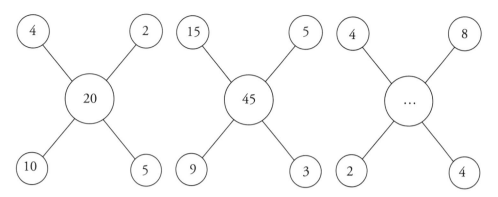

28. Find the missing number.

    6   3   9   12   21   ...   54   87

29. What is the missing number?

    12:24::....:14

    A. 13   B. 5   C. 6   D. 21   E. 7

30. Find the missing number.

    6   8   7   9   8   10   ...

31. Find the missing number.

    12   11   14   14   16   17   ...

32. Find the missing number.

    4   12   8

    13   9   ...

    9   7   8

33. Find the missing number.

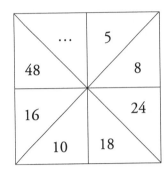

34. Find the missing number.

10   6   11   8   12   10   ...

35. Which number does not belong?

40   32   16   24   8   54   ...

36. Find the missing number.

8   3   10   12   21   32   52   ...

37. Find the missing number.

4   7   8   12   12   17   ...

38. Find the missing number.

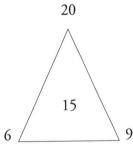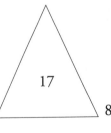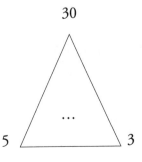

39. Find the missing number.

6   7   13   20   33   53   ...

40. Find the missing number.

7   14   2

4   20   ...

3   27   9

41. Find the missing number.

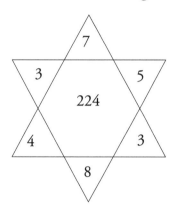 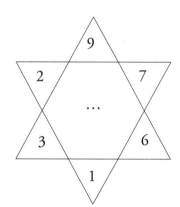

42. Find the missing number.

10   6   12   3   14   ...

43. Find the missing numbers.

15   (120)   4

13   (   )   5

9   (54)   12

10   (105)   21

8   (   )   7

44. Find the missing number.

5	7
9	6

9	5
2	11

3	8
15	...

45. Find the missing number.

48   82   44   77   40   72   ...

46. Find the missing number.

27   27   54   162   648   ...

47. Find the missing number.

321   (6)   231
555   ( )   285

48. Find the missing number.

7   4   6   6   5   8   4   ...

49. Find the missing number.

4   7   11   18   29   ...

50. Find the missing numbers.

8   15   22   29   ...   43   50

Answers

1. 44. (The inner number is equal to the sum of the outer numbers.)
2. 20. (The series alternately adds 3 and subtracts 2.)
3. 7. (Calculate the difference between the first and third numbers and divide the result by 2.)
4. 10. (There are two alternating series; the first increases by 2 and the second by 3.)
5. 23. (Calculate the sum of the first and second number, the second and third, the third and fourth, etc.)
6. The answer to the first puzzle is 75. (Calculate the sum of the first and third numbers.) The answer to the second puzzle is 9. (Multiply the outer numbers and divide the result by 2.)
7. E; 36. (Calculate the square.)
8. 22. (Multiply the first and second number, the second and third, etc., and add 1.)
9. 21. (The sum of each row is 48.)
10. 14. (It is double the number opposite.)
11. The answer to the first puzzle is 9. (There are two alternating series; the first decreases by 1 and the second increases by 2.) The answer to the second puzzle is 11. (Calculate the sum of the first and second numbers, the second and third, etc., and subtract 1.)
12. 4. (The third number is the sum of the first and second numbers.)
13. 27. (Multiply the outer numbers and divide the result by 2.)
14. 19. (The sum of the top numbers in the box is always equal to the sum of the bottom numbers.)
15. 64 and 71. (The series increases by 7.)
16. 31. (There are two alternating series; the first increases by 6 and the second by 3.)
17. 9. (The sum of the numbers is always 21.)
18. 18. (Multiply the numbers at the base of the triangle, then divide the result by the upper number.)
19. 6 and 2. (There are two alternating series; the first decreases by 2 and the second by 3.)

20. 82. (Calculate the sum of the first and second, the second and third, etc.)
21. 49. (Multiply the first and second number and add 1.)
22. 1. (There are two alternating series; the first increases by 2 and the second decreases by 1.)
23. 3. (The sum of the numbers in the rows is always 16.)
24. 24 and 27. (There are two alternating series; the first increases by 9 and the second by 8.)
25. C; 22. (The first number is half of the second number.)
26. 3. (The sum of the columns is 10.)
27. 16. (Multiply the numbers in the diagonals to get the number in the center.)
28. 33. (Calculate the sum of the first and second numbers, the second and third, etc.)
29. E; 7. (The first number is half of the second number.)
30. 9. (The series alternately adds 2 and subtracts 1.)
31. 18. (There are two alternating series; the first increases by 2 and the second by 3.)
32. 2. (The sum of each row is 24.)
33. 36. (From right to left, the number opposite is its double.)
34. 13. (There are two alternating series; the first increases by 1 and the second by 2.)
35. 54. (All of the other numbers are divisible by 4.)
36. 83. (Calculate the sum of the first and second numbers, the second and third, etc., and subtract 1.)
37. 16. (There are two alternating series; the first increases by 4 and the second by 5.)
38. 12. (The sum of the numbers in each triangle is always 50.)
39. 86. (Calculate the sum of the first and second numbers, the second and third, etc.)
40. 5. (Divide the second number by the first.)
41. 180. (Calculate the sum of the numbers of the two large triangles that form the star and multiply them.)
42. 0. (There are two alternating series; the first increases by 2 and the second decreases by 3.)

43. The answer to the first puzzle is 130. (Multiply the outer numbers and double the result.) The answer to the second puzzle is 28. (Multiply the outer numbers and divide by two.)

44. 1. (The sum of the numbers in the boxes is always 27.)

45. 36. (There are two alternating series; the first decreases by 4 and the second by 5.)

46. 3,240. (The series increases by multiplying successively by 1, 2, 3, 4, and 5.)

47. 15. (It's the sum of the individual digits of the number on either side.)

48. 10. (There are two alternating series; the first decreases by 1 and the second increases by 2.)

49. 47. (Calculate the sum of the first and second numbers, the second and third, etc.)

50. 36. (The series increases by 7.)

Spatial Test

1. Which figure does not belong?

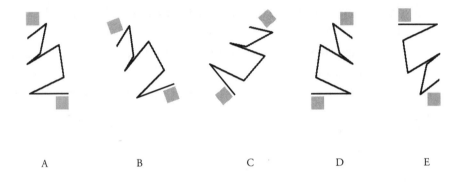

<table>
<tr><td>A</td><td>B</td><td>C</td><td>D</td><td>E</td></tr>
</table>

2. Which figure does not belong?

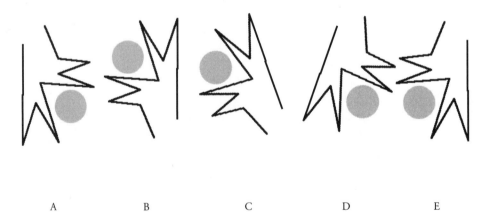

<table>
<tr><td>A</td><td>B</td><td>C</td><td>D</td><td>E</td></tr>
</table>

3. Which figure does not belong?

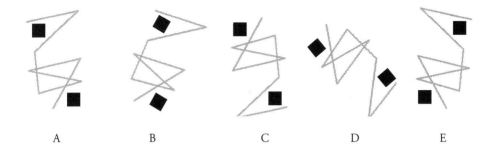

A   B   C   D   E

4. What is the next figure in the series?

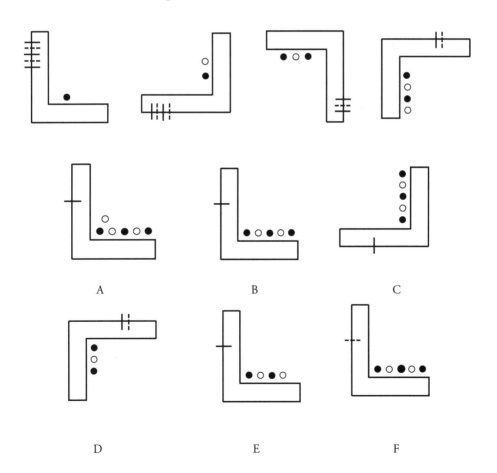

A   B   C

D   E   F

5. Insert the correct figure.

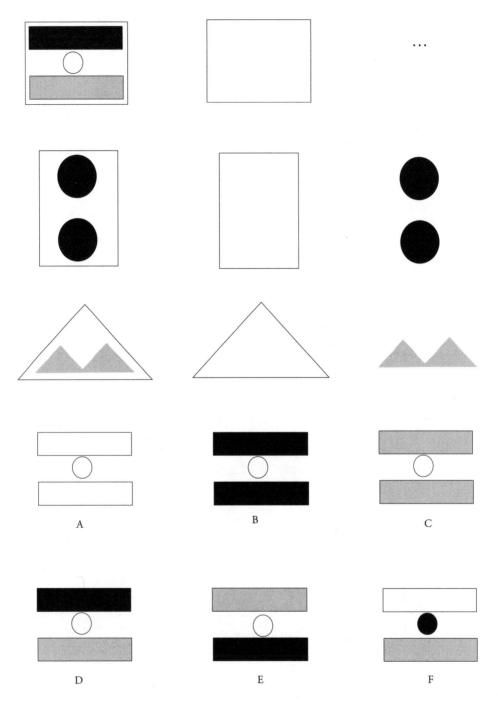

A

B

C

D

E

F

6. Which figure does not belong?

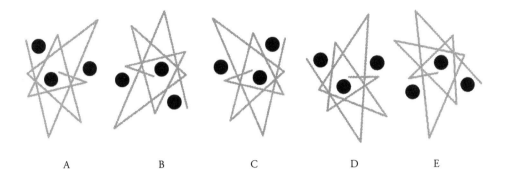

A   B   C   D   E

7. What is the next figure in the series?

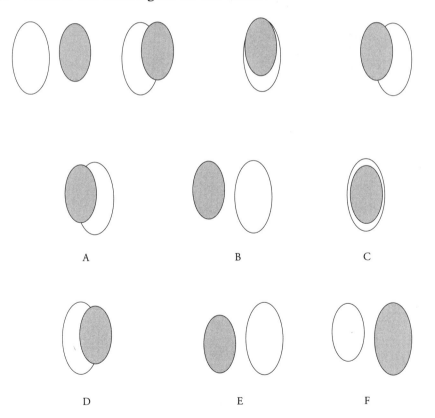

A   B   C

D   E   F

8. Insert the correct figure.

A

B

C

D

E

F

9. Which figure does not belong?

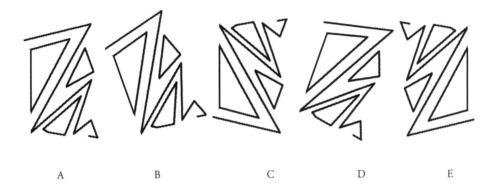

A   B   C   D   E

10. What is the next figure in the series?

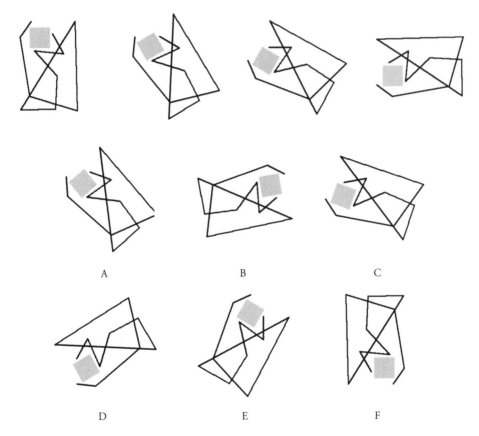

A   B   C

D   E   F

11. Insert the correct figure.

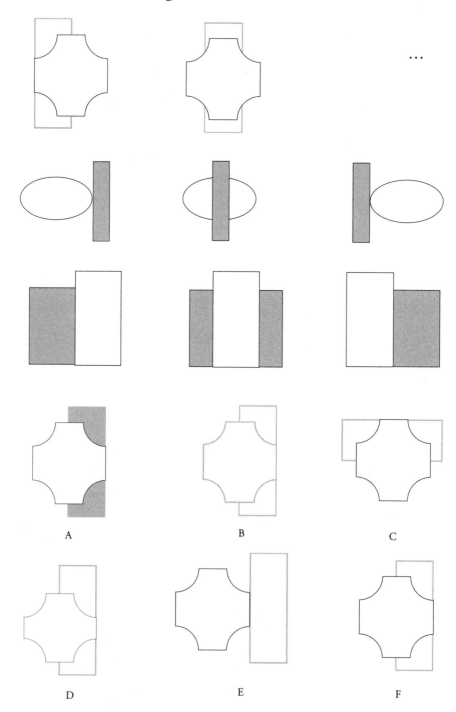

12. Which figure does not belong?

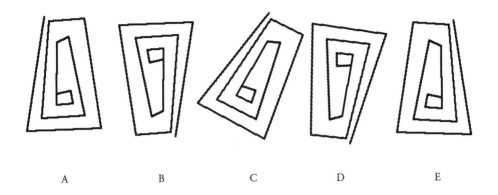

A   B   C   D   E

13. What is the next figure in the series?

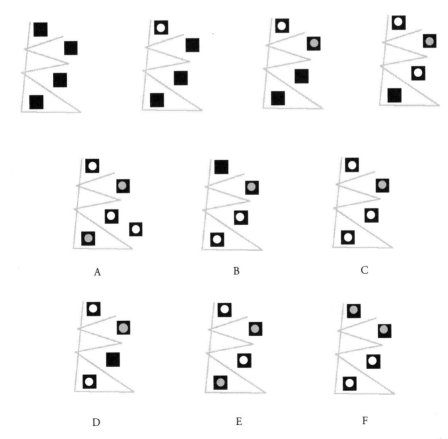

14. Which figure does not belong?

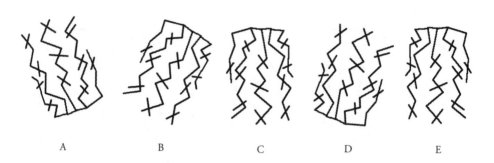

A   B   C   D   E

15. What is the next figure in the series?

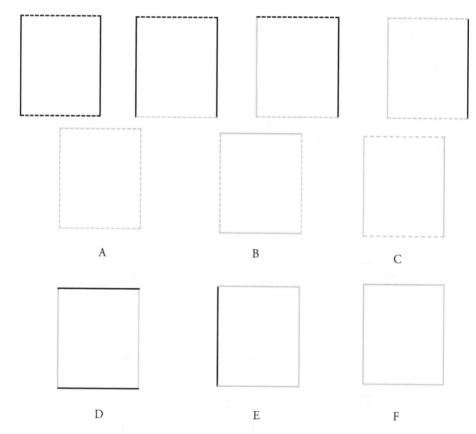

A   B   C

D   E   F

16. What is the missing figure?

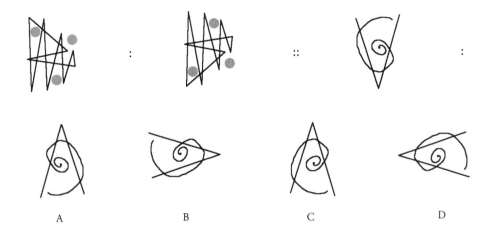

17. What is the next figure in the series?

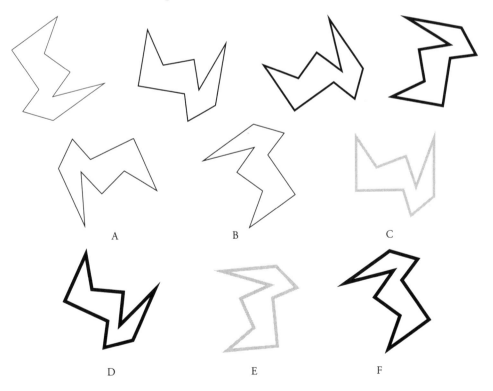

18. Insert the correct figure.

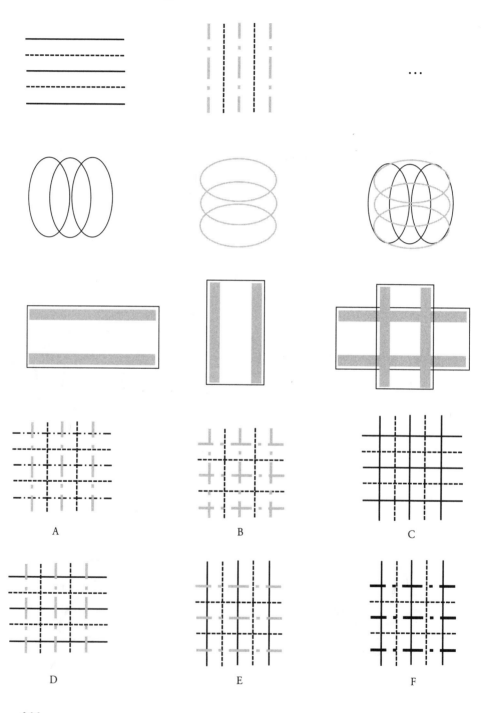

19. What is the missing figure?

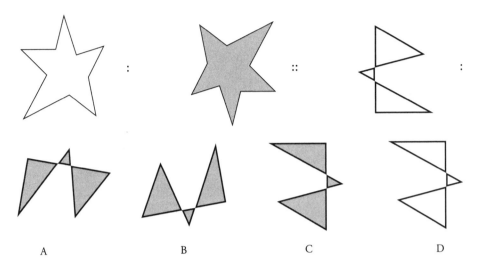

A   B   C   D

20. Which figure does not belong?

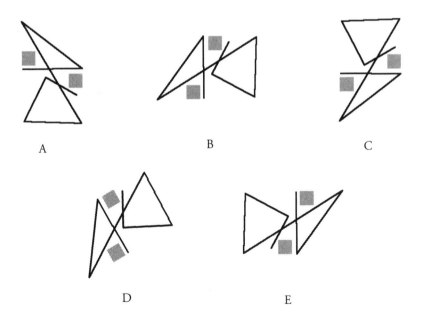

A   B   C

D   E

21. What is the next figure in the series?

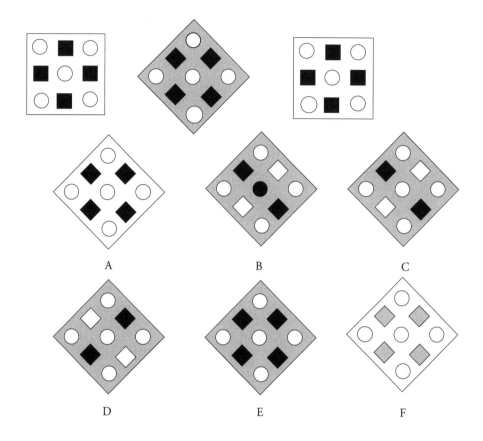

22. Which figure does not belong?

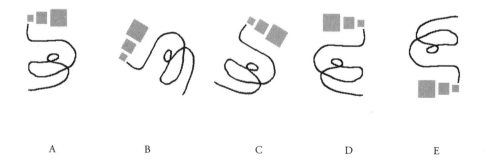

A   B   C   D   E

23. What is the missing figure?

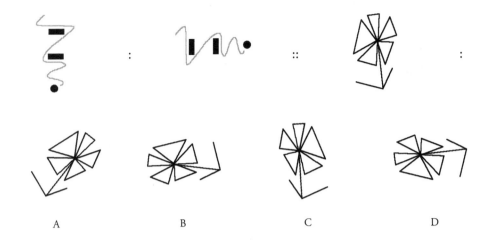

A   B   C   D

24. What is the next figure in the series?

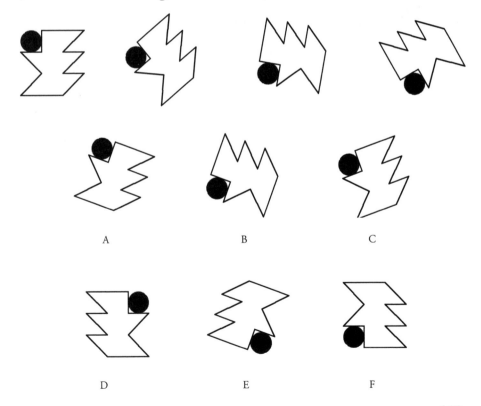

A   B   C

D   E   F

25. Insert the correct figure.

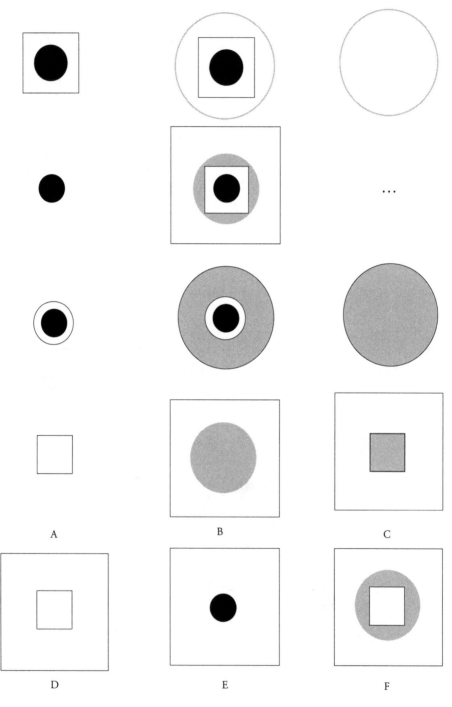

26. Which figure does not belong?

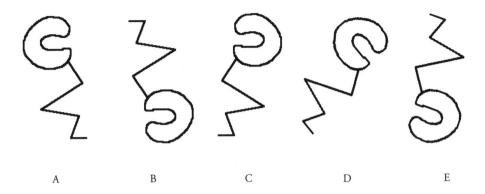

| A | B | C | D | E |

27. What is the next figure in the series?

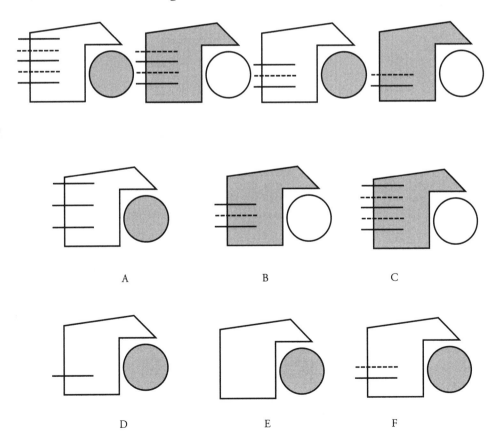

| A | B | C |

| D | E | F |

28. What is the next figure in the series?

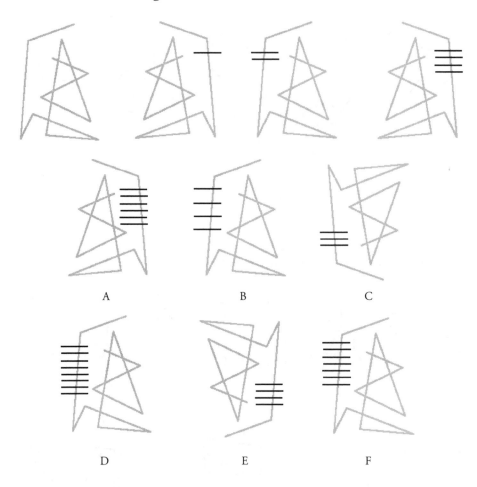

29. Which figure does not belong?

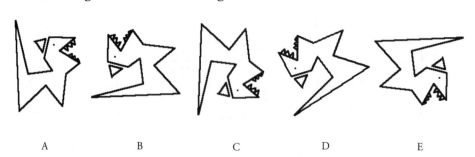

A   B   C   D   E

30. Which figure does not belong?

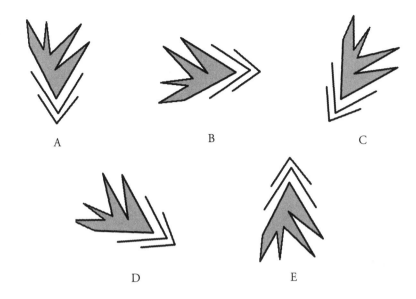

31. Which figure does not belong?

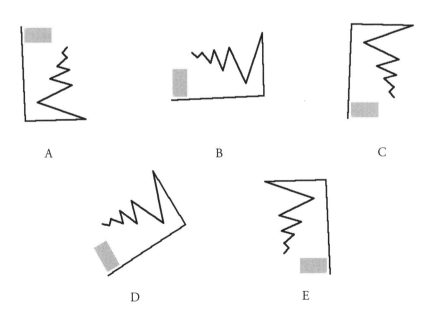

32. Insert the correct figure.

A

B

C

D

E

F

33. What is the next figure in the series?

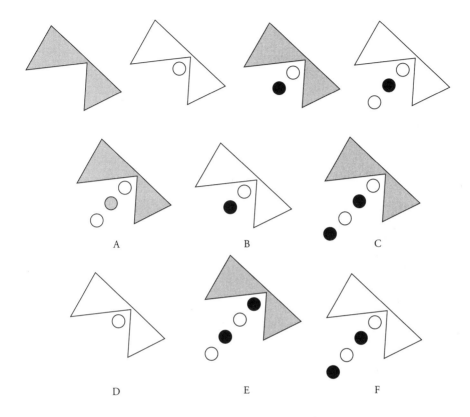

34. What is the missing figure?

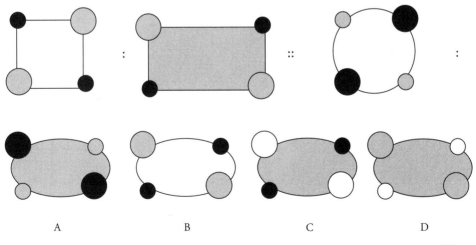

35. Insert the correct figure.

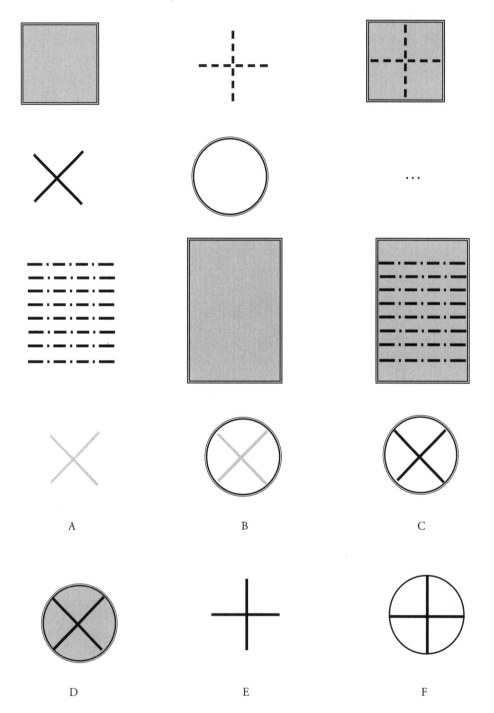

A   B   C

D   E   F

36. What is the next figure in the series?

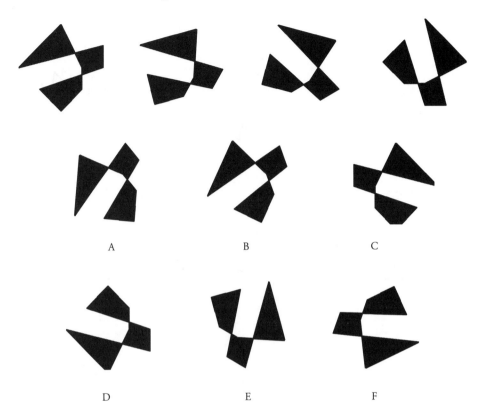

37. Which figure does not belong?

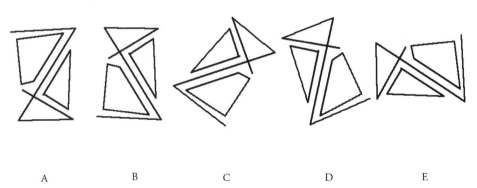

38. Which figure does not belong?

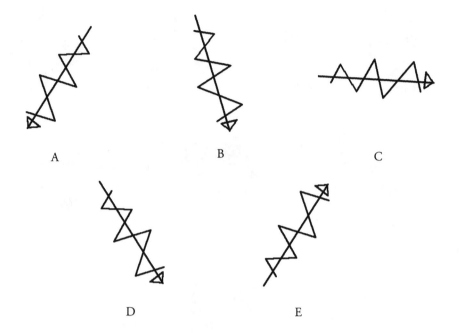

A

B

C

D

E

39. Which figure does not belong?

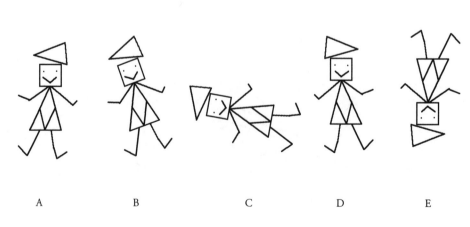

A   B   C   D   E

40. Insert the correct figure.

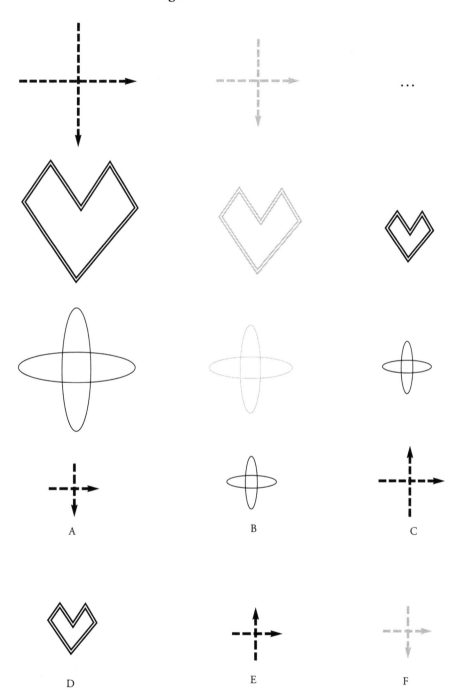

41. What is the next figure in the series?

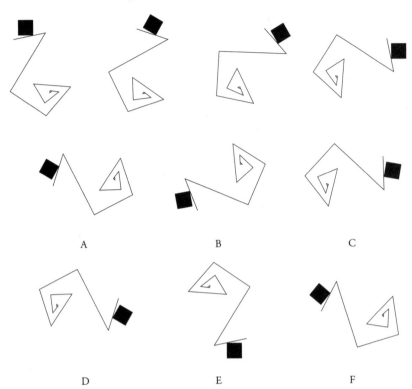

A   B   C

D   E   F

42. What is the missing figure?

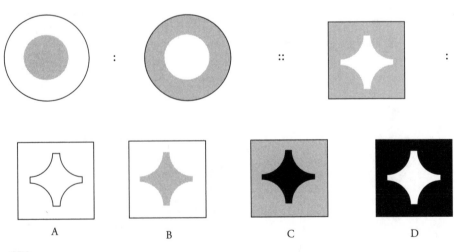

A   B   C   D

43. Insert the correct figure.

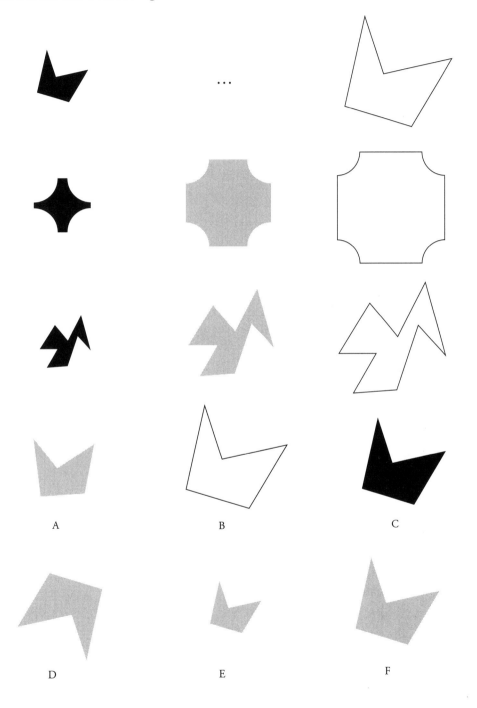

A

B

C

D

E

F

44. What is the next figure in the series?

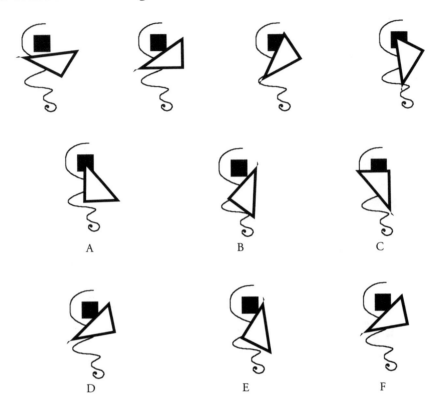

45. What is the missing figure?

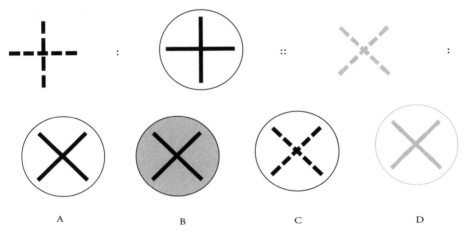

46. What is the next figure in the series?

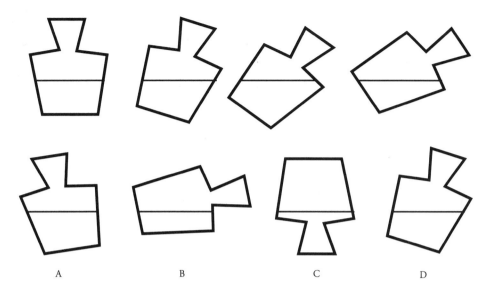

A   B   C   D

47. What is the next figure in the series?

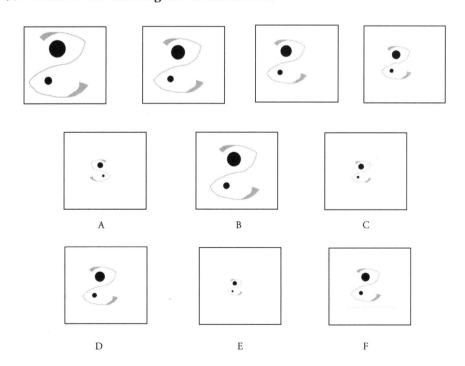

A   B   C

D   E   F

48. Insert the correct figure.

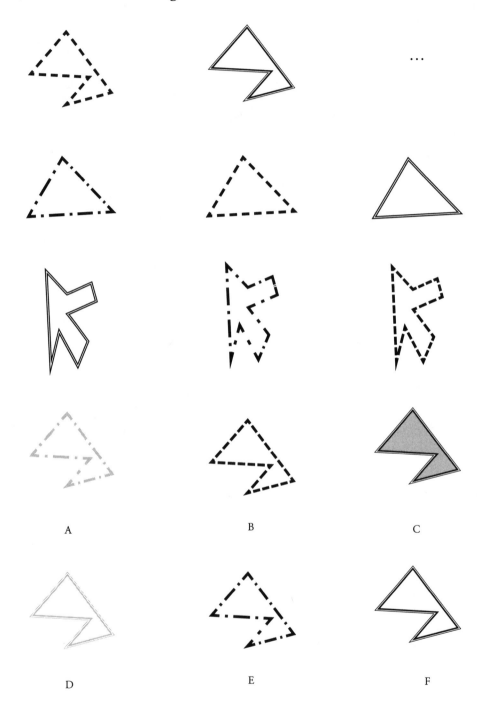

A

B

C

D

E

F

49. Which figure does not belong?

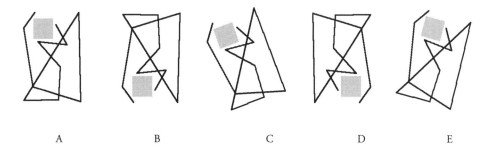

A   B   C   D   E

50. Which figure does not belong?

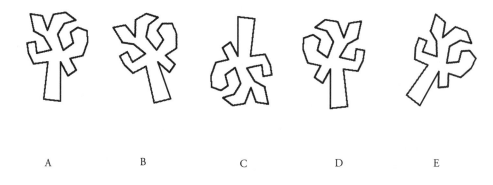

A   B   C   D   E

Answers

1. D. (The figure is reversed.)
2. E. (The figure is reversed.)
3. E. (The figure is reversed.)
4. B. (The figure rotates 90 degrees counterclockwise, adds a small circle, and eliminates a line.)
5. D. (Subtract the second figure from the first.)
6. C. (The figure is reversed.)
7. B. (The oval on top moves progressively leftward.)
8. F. (The lines progressively decrease in number and alternate between dashed and solid.)
9. C. (The figure is reversed.)
10. D. (The figure rotates 30 degrees counterclockwise.)
11. F. (The figure on top moves progressively leftward.)
12. E. (The figure is reversed.)
13. E. (Each successive figure adds a small circle, alternating between white and gray.)
14. E. (The figure is reversed.)
15. C. (The figure gradually turns gray.)
16. C. (The figure is upside down.)
17. F. (The figure rotates 45 degrees counterclockwise and the outline gets thicker.)
18. D. (The two figures overlap.)
19. C. (The figure rotates 180 degrees and becomes gray.)
20. C. (The figure is reversed.)
21. E. (The figure rotates 45 degrees and the background becomes gray.)
22. D. (The figure is reversed.)
23. B. (The figure is reversed and rotates 90 degrees counterclockwise.)
24. E. (The figure rotates counterclockwise each time.)
25. F. (Subtract the first figure from the second.)
26. C. (The figure is reversed.)
27. D. (The figure alternates between white and gray and successively eliminates a line.)
28. D. (The figure reverses each time, and the number of black lines doubles.)

29. C. (The figure is reversed.)
30. E. (The figure is reversed.)
31. C. (The figure is reversed.)
32. A. (The figure alternates between white, black, and gray and rotates counterclockwise.)
33. C. (The figure alternates between white and gray and adds one small circle each time.)
34. A. (The figure is stretched out, becomes gray, and the gray and black dots switch locations.)
35. C. (Combine the first and second figures of each series.)
36. E. (The figure rotates 30 degrees clockwise.)
37. B. (The figure is reversed.)
38. D. (The figure is reversed.)
39. D. (The figure is reversed.)
40. A. (The figure gets smaller from left to right and alternates between black and gray.)
41. D. (The figure rotates 30 degrees clockwise.)
42. B. (The colors switch between the two figures.)
43. F. (The figure gradually gets larger and alternates between black, gray, and white.)
44. C. (The inner triangle rotates counterclockwise.)
45. D. (The figure becomes solid and a circle is placed around it.)
46. B. (The figure rotates clockwise.)
47. C. (The internal figure gradually gets smaller.)
48. E. (The figures alternate between broken lines, double lines, and dotted lines.)
49. B. (The figure is reversed.)
50. D. (The figure is reversed.)

Verbal Test

1. Unscramble the following letters to find the animal that is not a mammal.

A. plodnih
B. zaphimceen
C. anagiu
D. firfage
E. yootce

2. What is the missing word?

April:spring::October:...

A. winter
B. autumn
C. summer
D. year
E. December

3. Find the word that means the same thing as each of the other two.

Sanctuary (....) Marmalade

4. Complete the series with the correct word.

Futurism
Expressionism
Surrealism
Dadaism
...

A. Impressionism   B. picture   C. avant garde   D. manifesto
E. Bauhaus

5. **Which two words are similar?**

   A. sun   B. wheel   C. hole   D. banana   E. pencil

6. **Which name does not belong?**

   A. Baudelaire
   B. Mallarme
   C. Keats
   D. Verlaine
   E. Rimbaud

7. **Unscramble the following letters to find the word that is not a city.**

   A. rpais
   B. lmina
   C. ercfna
   D. irtnu
   E. evince

8. **Which word is not a synonym of the others?**

   A. nurture
   B. nourish
   C. feed
   D. supply
   E. inculcate

9. **Choose the correct response.**

   Indigo is the prettiest color.

   A. definitely true
   B. not true
   C. sometimes true
   D. an opinion

10. **Which word does not belong?**

   A. oak   B. sunflower   C. maple   D. poplar   E. beech

11. Which two animals are similar?

A. vulture   B. iguana   C. whale   D. lion   E. dolphin

12. Find the word that means the same thing as each of the other two.

Detail (....) Particular

13. Unscramble the following letters to find the word that is not a school subject.

A.   smoccione
B.   getmyreo
C.   rurelateit
D.   histemcry
E.   facetarie

14. Which word is not a synonym of the others?

A.   uninterested
B.   indifferent
C.   dispassionate
D.   energetic
E.   apathetic

15. Complete the series with the correct word.

Dance
Diet
Dream
Drink
...
A. decode   B. diagnose   C. drop   D. devour   E. dribble

16. Which two words are similar?

A. Saturn   B. sky   C. horizontal   D. Venus   E. sun

17. What is the missing word?

While:adverb::be:...

A. subject
B. verb
C. adjective
D. word
E. noun

18. Unscramble the following letters to find the name that is not a man's.

A. naxelared
B. nadon
C. roegeg
D. akrm
E. rahcird

19. Find the word that means the same thing as each of the other two.

Alias (....) Knob

20. Which mountain range does not belong?

A. Appalachian
B. Pyrenees
C. Blue Ridge
D. Sierra Nevada
E. Adirondack

21. Which two animals are similar?

A. centipede　　B. penguin　　C. shark　　D. iguana　　E. seagull

22. Which term is the most appropriate?

Ecclesiastical district under the jurisdiction of a bishop.

A. Vatican　　B. diocese　　C. parish

23. What is the missing word?

Black:negro::green:…

A. amarillo
B. verde
C. blanco
D. rojo
E. azul

24. Unscramble the following letters to find the word that is not a fruit.

A. rawrystreb
B. shuqas
C. ringeneat
D. meltawnero
E. pleapinep

25. Choose the correct response.

Some animals are not mammals.

A. definitely true
B. not true
C. sometimes true
D. an opinion

26. Which word is not a synonym of the others?

A. mar
B. carve
C. ruin
D. damage
E. spoil

27. Which two words are similar?

A. tennis   B. race car driving   C. basketball   D. skiing
E. fencing

28. What is the missing name?

Laura:Petrarch::Beatrice:...

A. Cervantes
B. Dante
C. Boccaccio
D. Goethe
E. Joyce

29. Unscramble the following letters to find the word that is not a profession.

A. tidroe
B. tophogrephar
C. iloras
D. atabsoli
E. riname

30. Which word does not belong?

A. square
B. circle
C. rectangle
D. pyramid
E. octagon

31. What is the missing word?

Man:masculine::woman:...

A. wife
B. mom
C. feminine
D. girl
E. femininity

32. Find the word that means the same thing as each of the other two.

Postpone (....) Chart

33. Unscramble the following letters to find the name that is not a constellation.

A. scpeis
B. usagsep
C. porciso
D. ultop
E. isacaposei

34. What is the missing sign?

lion:Leo::scales:...

A. Sagittarius
B. Libra
C. Gemini
D. Capricorn
E. Pisces

35. Which two words are similar?

A. go   B. always   C. rejoice   D. Frances   E. tasty

36. What is the missing word?

Fat:thin::high:...

A. brief
B. low
C. small
D. narrow
E. under

37. Unscramble the following letters to find the word that is not a color.

A. lwoeyl
B. elub
C. ogidin
D. trinethe
E. gnatema

38. **Which location does not belong?**

    A. Yellowstone
    B. Everglades
    C. Oregon Caves
    D. Yosemite
    E. Grand Teton

39. **Which two words are similar?**

    A. hurricane   B. depression   C. tornado   D. wind   E. torpedo

40. **Complete the series with the correct word.**

    Garnet
    Ruby
    Sapphire
    Emerald
    ...
    A. Amber   B. Jade   C. Quartz   D. Amethyst   E. Onyx

41. **Unscramble the following letters to find the word that is not an occupation.**

    A. yctaaur
    B. okoc
    C. twerir
    D. sittar
    E. cnelip

42. **Choose the correct response.**

    The Nile flows from North to South.

    A. definitely true
    B. not true
    C. sometimes true
    D. an opinion

43. Which term is the most appropriate?

Not influenced by preconceptions, passions, or subjective interests.

A. level-headed   B. objective   C. correct

44. Find the word that means the same thing as each of the other two.

Shrink (....) Agreement

45. Which word is not a synonym of the others?

A. impish
B. puckish
C. staid
D. mischievous
E. playful

46. Unscramble the following letters to find the word that is not an electrical appliance.

A. sivletenio
B. mharrica
C. warhes
D. denrelb
E. saridshewh

47. Which two cities are similar?

A. Milan   B. Melbourne   C. Memphis   D. Montevideo
E. Munich

48. Choose the correct response.

All roads lead to Rome.

A. definitely true
B. not true
C. sometimes true
D. an opinion

49. Find the word that means the same thing as each of the other two.

Canal (....) Station

50. Which word is not a synonym of the others?

    A.   contemporary
    B.   antiquated
    C.   archaic
    D.   outdated
    E.   antediluvian

Answers

1. C; iguana. (This is a reptile; dolphin, chimpanzee, giraffe, and coyote are mammals.)
2. B; autumn.
3. Preserve.
4. A; Impressionism. (They are all art movements.)
5. D and E, banana and pencil, respectively. (Each has six letters.)
6. C; Keats. (He is not a French poet.)
7. C; France. (This is a country; Paris, Milan, Turin, and Venice are cities.)
8. E; inculcate.
9. D.
10. B; sunflower. (It's a flower, not a tree.)
11. C and E, whale and dolphin, respectively. (Both are marine mammals.)
12. Specific.
13. E; cafeteria. (This is a location; economics, geometry, literature, and chemistry are all subjects.)
14. D; energetic.
15. C; drop. (The words are in alphabetical order.)
16. A and D, Saturn and Venus, respectively. (Both are planets.)
17. B; verb.
18. B; Donna. (This is a woman's name; Alexander, George, Mark, and Richard are men's names.)
19. Handle.
20. B; Pyrenees. (This is a mountain range in Europe; the others are all North American mountain ranges.)
21. B and E, penguin and seagull, respectively. (Both are birds.)
22. B; diocese.
23. B; verde.
24. B; squash. (This is a vegetable; strawberry, tangerine, watermelon, and pineapple are fruits.)
25. A.
26. B; carve.

27. A and C, tennis and basketball, respectively. (Both are sports that use a ball.)
28. B; Dante.
29. D; sailboat. (This is an object; editor, photographer, sailor, and marine are professions.)
30. D; pyramid. (The other figures are all two-dimensional.)
31. C; feminine.
32. Table.
33. D; Pluto. (This is a planet; Pisces, Pegasus, Scorpio, and Cassiopeia are constellations.)
34. B; Libra.
35. A and C, go and rejoice, respectively. (Both are verbs.)
36. B; low.
37. D; thirteen. (This is a number; yellow, blue, indigo, and magenta are colors.)
38. C; Oregon Caves. (This is a national monument; the others are all national parks.)
39. A and C, hurricane and tornado, respectively. (They are both natural disasters.)
40. D; Amethyst. (They are all birthstones.)
41. E; pencil. (This is an object; actuary, cook, writer, and artist are occupations.)
42. B.
43. B; objective.
44. Contract.
45. C; staid.
46. B; armchair. (This is furniture; television, washer, blender, and dishwasher are electronic appliances.)
47. A and E, Milan and Munich, respectively. (Both are European cities.)
48. B.
49. Channel.
50. A; contemporary.

Advanced Test

1. What is the missing word?

England:English::Brazil:...

A. Spanish
B. French
C. Portuguese
D. Latin
E. Russian

2. Find the missing number.

1   4   5   9   9   14   13   19   ...

3. Unscramble the following letters to find the name that is not an inventor.

A. klifnarn
B. grentebug
C. ratpuse
D. iaconmr
E. totserail

4. Find the missing number.

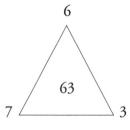 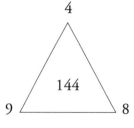 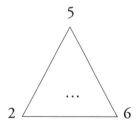

5. **What is the next figure in the series?**

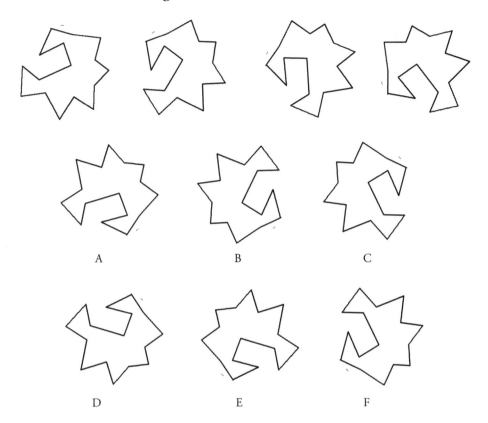

6. **Find the missing number.**

1   3   4   13   ...

7. **Complete the series with the correct word.**

cello
guitar
piano
violin
...

A. trombone   B. xylophone   C. drum   D. trumpet
E. saxophone

8. Find the missing number.

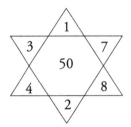 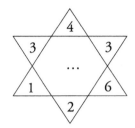

9. Find the missing numbers.

8-4-9   14-5-2   18-1-...

10. Find the word that means the same thing as each of the other two.

Acquaintance (....) Call

11. Find the missing number.

3   6   8   13   20   32   ...

12. Choose the correct response.

Planets move in circular orbits.

A.   definitely true
B.   not true
C.   sometimes true
D.   an opinion

13. Find the missing number.

93   (12)   75

104   (5)   23

62   ( )   44

14. Which word is not a synonym of the others?

A. adjudicate
B. arbitrate
C. mediate
D. provoke
E. referee

15. Find the missing number.

3   1   2   1   1   ...

16. Which word is not a synonym of the others?

A. beat
B. whip
C. lash
D. soothe
E. thrash

17. Find the missing number.

F-O-R   T-A-R   P-U-...

18. Which two words are similar?

A. hexagon   B. apple   C. orangutan   D. sailboat   E. telephone

19. Which figure does not belong?

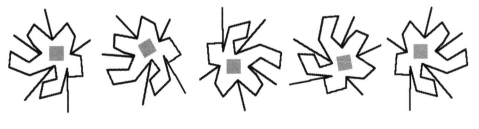

A   B   C   D   E

20. Find the missing word.

Homer: Odyssey::Vergil:...

A. Iliad
B. Aeneid
C. Metamorphoses
D. Theogony
E. Oresteia

21. Find the missing number.

57-15-12   68-20-8   24-...-12

22. Which of the following is not a Nobel Laureate?

A. Rosalind Franklin
B. Francis Crick
C. Mother Teresa
D. James Watson
E. Aung San Suu Kyi

23. Which figure does not belong?

A

B

C

D

E

24. What is the next figure in the series?

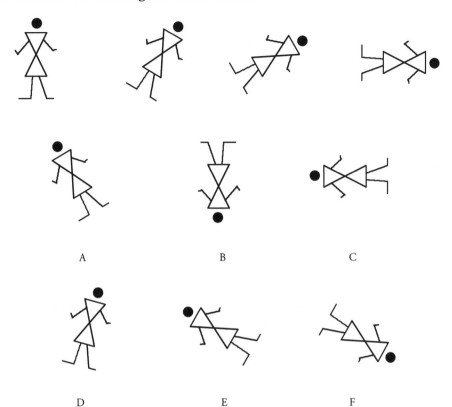

A   B   C

D   E   F

25. Complete the series with the correct word.

boy
door
flame
raisin
...
A. pole   B. imprudent   C. tailor   D. sardine   E. cylinder

26. Find the missing number.

11   48   9   45   7   42   5   ...

27. Find the missing number.

6	3
1	4

9	4
2	1

24	3
1	...

28. Choose the correct response.

All squares are rectangles.

A. definitely true
B. not true
C. sometimes true
D. an opinion

29. Find the missing number.

48   82   44   77   40   72   ...

30. Find the word that means the same thing as each of the other two.

Decline (....) Garbage

31. Find the missing number.

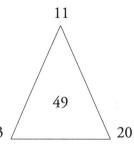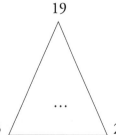

32. Unscramble the following letters to find a woman who was not a Queen.

A. sealib
B. abethizel
C. tearbix
D. nadia
E. yarm

33. Which two animals are similar?

A. ladybug   B. eagle   C. turtle   D. jackdaw   E. tiger

34. Which figure does not belong?

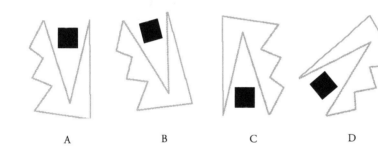

A   B   C   D   E

35. Which number does not belong?

18   60   56   42   12   96

36. Find the word that means the same thing as each of the other two.

Eligible (....) Restrict

37. Find the missing number.

9   5   15   8   21   ...   27   14

38. What is the next figure in the series?

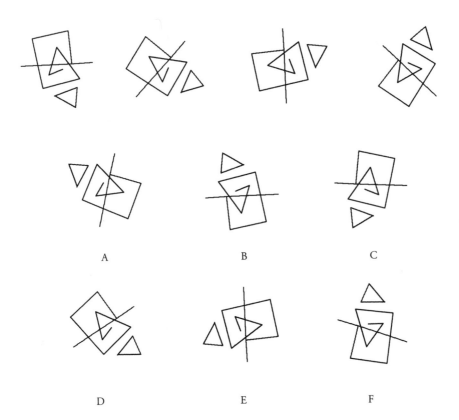

A   B   C

D   E   F

39. What is the missing number?

8:16::32:...

A. 12   B. 24   C. 18   D. 64   E. 120

40. Which word is not a synonym of the others?

A. credulous
B. gullible
C. shrewd
D. naive
E. unsuspecting

41. Find the missing number.

9   5   13   10   17   ...   21   20

42. Find the word that means the same thing as each of the other two.

Hollow (....) Cavity

43. Find the missing letter.

F   K   P   ...   Z

44. Find the missing number.

11   7   10   5   9   3   ...

45. Which figure does not belong?

A   B   C

D   E

46. Find the missing number.

   6   9   8   6   10   3   12   ...

47. Choose the correct response.

All cats have tails.

A. definitely true
B. not true
C. sometimes true
D. an opinon

48. What is the next figure in the series?

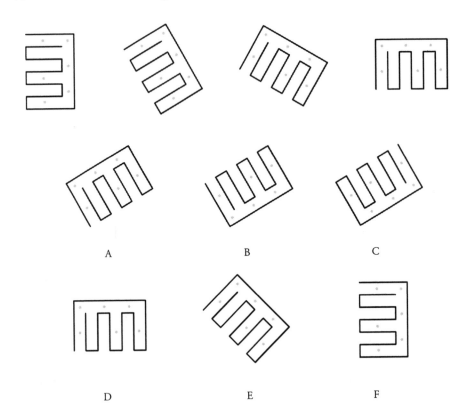

A   B   C

D   E   F

49. Find the missing number.

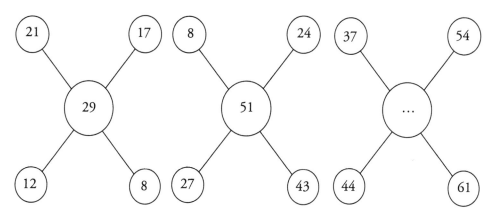

50. Find the missing number.

400	(5)	80
208	(52)	4
976	( )	122

Answers

1. C; Portuguese.
2. 17. (There are two alternating series; the first increases by 4 and the second by 5.)
3. E; Aristotle. (He is a philosopher; Franklin, Gutenberg, Pasteur, and Marconi are inventors.)
4. 30. (Calculate the product of the numbers outside the triangle and divide the result by 2.)
5. E. (The figure rotates counterclockwise.)
6. 53. (Calculate the product of the first and second number, the second and third, etc., and add 1.)
7. B; xylophone. (The words are in alphabetical order.)
8. 38. (Calculate the sum of the outer numbers and multiply the result by 2.)
9. 2. (The sum of the numbers is always 21.)
10. Contact.
11. 51. (Calculate the sum of the first and second number, the second and third number, etc., and subtract 1.)
12. B. (Planets move in eliptical orbits.)
13. 8. (It's the sum of the individual digits of each outside number.)
14. D; provoke.
15. 0. (Calculate the product of the first and second number, the second and third number, etc., and subtract 1.)
16. D; soothe.
17. B. (The sum of the numerical equivalents of each series of letters is 39.)
18. C and E, orangutan and telephone, respectively. (They both have 9 letters.)
19. E. (The figure is reversed.)
20. B; Aeneid.
21. 4. (Calculate the difference between the first and third numbers in the series and divide by 3.)
22. A; Rosalind Franklin.
23. C. (The figure is reversed.)
24. F. (The figure always rotates 30 degrees clockwise.)

25. D; sardine. (The words are in alphabetical order and their length increases by 1 letter.)
26. 39. (There are two alternating series; the first decreases by 2 and the second by 3.)
27. 1. (The product of the numbers in each square is always 72.)
28. A.
29. 36. (There are two alternating series; the first decreases by 4 and the second by 5.)
30. Refuse.
31. 44. (Calculate the product of the numbers in the lower angles and subtract the number in the upper angle.)
32. D; Diana. (She was a princess; Isabel, Elizabeth, Beatrix, and Mary were Queens.)
33. B and D, eagle and jackdaw, respectively. (Both are types of birds.)
34. E. (The figure is reversed.)
35. 56. (It's the only number not divisible by 6.)
36. Qualify.
37. 11. (There are two alternating series; the first increases by 6 and the second by 3.)
38. B. (The figure rotates 45 degrees counterclockwise.)
39. D; 64. (The second number is the double of the first number.)
40. C; shrewd.
41. 15. (There are two alternating series; the first increases by 4 and the second by 5.)
42. Empty.
43. U. (The series always skips 4 letters.)
44. 8. (There are two alternating series; the first decreases by 1 and the second by 2.)
45. E. (The figure is reversed.)
46. 0. (There are two alternating series; the first increases by two and the second decreases by 3.)
47. B.
48. A. (The figure rotates 30 degrees counterclockwise.)
49. 98. (It's the sum of each diagonal.)
50. 8. (It's the first number divided by the third number.)